The prayer of silence is in reality a call to
beckons us to find a sacred place to allow
spirit of God.

Jim Filbeck, Secretary/Treasurer, MN Dist. ... the Assemblies of God

In the age of brokenness all around us, this research on contemplative prayer brings the vision of wholeness in our lives and also the world we live and engage with every day. The world, which is filled with loud noises competing for our attention even in Christian spirituality, the author convinces us of the power of stillness as a means of embodiment in multiple dimensions.

Wonsuk Ma, Executive Director, Center for Spirit-Empowered Research, Distinguished Professor of Global Christianity, Oral Roberts University

This author brings to our attention the importance of Christian Contemplative Prayer through which individuals and communities commune with God in his divine ineffable loving presence. Such prayers bring us to a deeper self-understanding and self-awareness in our embodied selves before God and help us to relate to other people and God's creation with a holistic sense of well-being (Shalom). The book will encourage the readers to practise such life-transforming prayers.

Damon So, Research Tutor, Oxford Centre for Mission Studies

Within all walks of life there is an increasing concern for human wellbeing. This book, based on participant research, offers insight into the role of contemplative prayer in supporting wellbeing that is holistic: spiritual, physical, relational and environmental.

Jane Leach, Principal, Wesley House, University of Cambridge

In a world of noise (cars, bombings, people voicing their needs, rights and complaints), Kathy Holley invites the reader to contemplate the prayer of silence. This time of quietness is a mean to contemplate the One who is in "the still small voice" 1 Kings 19:12b. I appreciate this book that makes a difference between Christian spiritual discipline of meditation with eastern religious transcendental meditation found in Hinduism and Buddhism. This is a must-read book.

Philemon Salam SABA, Pastor New Life,
Assemblies of God Burkina Faso

Kathy Holley's work offers a significant corrective to the traditional evangelical suspicion of contemplative prayer. Through listening to the experience of Christian practitioners, she enables the reader to explore and engage with the riches of apophatic prayer from an orthodox perspective.

Rev Canon Dr Adrian Chatfield

Dr Kathleen Holley has written a tremendous book that addresses a topic that is critical for the follower of Christ. *The Prayer of Silence* speaks of waiting on the lord, prayerful meditation, and the practice of silence when praying. The discipline of being silent for short and long lengths of time enables the Christian to clear their thoughts so that the Holy Spirit can be heard with better clarity. Her historical research highlights the centuries of godly people who have demonstrated this discipline. All of us desperately need to hear the clear – wonderful direction that the Holy Spirit freely gives. "Those who wait on the Lord shall renew their strength." (Isaiah 40:31)

Wayde Goodall, author

We have much to learn about the impact of prayer on the life of the practitioner. Kathleen Holley provides a scholarly approach and insights into Christian Contemplative prayer, walking the reader through the evolution of the practice, and through her own qualitative research and analysis developed theoretical frameworks for understanding the interrelated dimensions of Christian Contemplative prayer as it relates to the practitioner. Holley's work advances our understandings of contemplative prayer practices, the impact on the practitioner's well-being and on the practitioner's relational understanding of God. This book is a valuable read for scholars, spiritual directors, ministry leaders, and seminary students.

Reverend Todd Wright,
Chaplain Evangelical Lutheran Church in America

The ancient practice of contemplative prayer has experienced a resurgence in recent years making it worthy of study. Kathleen Holley offers insight into contemplative prayer, discovering how the practice is embodied and the many benefits it brings. Holley shines light on an ancient Christian prayer practice with a contemporary twist.

Peter Althouse, Oral Roberts University

This little study on contemplative prayer is a wonderful contribution to the understanding of the role of embodiment, with all its dimensions, in our spiritual practice.

Marco Schorlemmer, WCCM coordinator and scientist

Too many of us are feeling preoccupied with unsettling anxiety that define our existence. Kathy Holley's writing on *The Prayer of Silence* is an important antidote for our divided lives that beckons us into deeper levels of God's grace and holistic well-being which he intended.

Roger Heuser, Professor of Leadership Studies at Vanguard University

This book starts out with a thorough though brief summary of the Christian contemplative history that situates it within the tradition starting in the early days of the followers of Jesus. While contemplative prayer may be new to modern day Christians, it is not new within the Christian tradition. Because Kathy interviewed so many long-time practitioners and ultimately started her own contemplative practice, she brings a familiar description of the fruits of contemplative prayer in modern language:

"This Christian embodied prayer practice can influence a holistic well-being (body, mind, and spirit) within the long-term practitioner," in addition to fostering "a greater awareness of the presence of God." I felt as if I was reading about my own long-time experience with contemplative prayer. She notes that because Christian contemplative prayer has only been brought back into the mainstream in the last 50 or so years, there is not much academic research like there is in some of the Eastern meditation traditions (Buddhism, mindfulness). As contemplative practices continue to grow in modern times, more attention needs to be paid to research to bring together ancient Christian contemplative prayer with modern science. This book highlights that need and is a good start!

Julie Saad, author of Contemplative Life: Discovering Our Path into the Heart of God

The Prayer of Silence

About the Author

Kathy Holley (PhD) is a speaker, educator, and retreat leader of Christian Contemplative Prayer: The Prayer of Silence. She is also the founder of *Wellbeing in Nature NW* where, as a certified Forest Therapy guide, she educates and guides others through the holistic wellbeing benefits of forest immersion experiences.

The Prayer of Silence

A Grounded Theory Exploration of Well-Being and Embodiment within Christian Spirituality

Kathy Holley

regnum

First published 2023 by Regnum Books International

This book is an abridged version of Kathleen Holley's thesis, "Christian contemplative prayer: a grounded theory exploration of well-being and embodiment within Christian spirituality" (PhD thesis, Middlesex University / Oxford Centre for Mission Studies).

Regnum is an imprint of the Oxford Centre for Mission Studies
St. Philip and St. James Church
Woodstock Road, Oxford OX2 6HR, UK
https://www.regnumbooks.net/

British Library Cataloguing in Publication Data. A catalogue record for this book is available from the British Library.

ISBN: 979-8-3419-0001-1
eBook ISBN: 979-8-3419-0002-8

Typeset in Candara by Words by Design.

Photo by Adrien Ledoux www.unsplash.com

All Scripture references are from the New International Version (NIV) unless they are contained (and referenced) in a quotation or otherwise noted.

The publication of this volume is made possible through the financial assistance of Evangelisches Missionswerk.

Distributed by Fortress Press in the US, Canada, India, and Brazil

Dedication

To our omnipresent God
and
each of this study's
36 Christian Contemplative Prayer practitioners
who so faithfully rest in God's presence.

~To God Be the Glory~

Contents

Acknowledgements

In considering acknowledgements, I am reminded of the scriptural verse:

Walk with the wise and become wise (Proverbs 13:20a).

This undertaking has been a journey of walking with those who have generously shared their insights, experience, and wisdom with me. This book is a condensed treatise of the original thesis, completed in June 2022, for which I am grateful to the faculty and staff at the Oxford Centre for Mission Studies for their academic guidance, the University of Oxford's Bodleian libraries for their superb resources, and the Middlesex University in London, England for its institutional support. I am also most appreciative to my two thesis supervisors: Peter Althouse, PhD, from Oral Roberts University and Reverend Adrian Chatfield, PhD, from Cambridge University, whose encouraging insights helped me to grow beyond my own understanding, and to Professor David Cranston, MB, ChB, DPhil, from the University of Oxford, who was instrumental in helping to reduce a lengthy thesis into a mini book. Lastly, but of utmost importance throughout this research project, thanks are due to my amazing mom, Erna; my wonderfully supportive husband, Russ; my two delightful daughters, Kristi (together with her husband, Jairus) and Rachel; and my two dear nieces, Emma and Heather, with whom I am wiser for having walked this journey of family together. Thank you does not begin to express my gratefulness to each one mentioned here.

Of course, this book (or its associated thesis) would not have been possible without all of my informative and wonderful participants. Their willingness to share their Christian Contemplative Prayer practice has been invaluable. I have been blessed by their knowledge, lived experience, and spiritual insights as they have so enthusiastically shared themselves and their time with me... with us. Thank you.

The silent prayer practice of Christian Contemplative Prayer is where ordinary prayer becomes perfect.

Cuthbert Butler, Benedictine abbot and scholar

1. Introduction

He says, "Be still and know that I am God... ". Psalm 46:10

In the Christian tradition, contemplative prayer is enlightened by Scripture and ancient church practices and is currently receiving renewed attention and global growth as a Christian spirituality discipline. Christian Contemplative Prayer promotes an intentional, inner silent awareness of God's presence. This is not to be confused with an emptying of the mind, but rather a silencing of all the mental chatter – placing one's focus on God. Quieting one's mental activity can be challenging, yet it is simply a process of 'letting go' of the inner thoughts that arise. While various approaches might exhibit similar methods of quieting one's self, Christian Contemplative Prayer centres on God's presence within an intentional silent space, thereby distinguishing it from other forms of meditation, spiritual practices, or the popular understanding of mindfulness.[1] This Christian embodied prayer practice can influence a holistic well-being (body, mind, and spirit) within the long-term practitioner.

---

[1] Mindfulness is a practice that is rooted in Buddhist teachings and philosophy, and incorporates theories related to attention to the present and practices which reinforce self-directed attentiveness.

Prayers can be recognized primarily as *kataphatic* or *apophatic*. Kataphatic prayer (Greek: *kataphasis*) is recognized as 'affirmation' and utilizes more mental thought processes such as words, images, reasoning, imagination, or maybe even memory. Apophatic prayer (Greek: *apophasis*) is attributed more towards 'negation', with its wordless shifting of one's attention away from the external and towards a more internal focus. This can feel a bit like emptiness or nothingness; however, apophatic prayer is not empty but rather it uses one's more subtle spiritual senses of perception. In the end, kataphatic and apophatic prayer can bring Christians to a greater awareness of God's presence, with Christian Contemplative Prayer being more closely related to the apophatic form of prayer.

Scholars recognize Christian Contemplative Prayer's historical development in various ways, including writings found within the Old and New Testaments; Jesus' life and teachings; the lived examples of Desert Fathers and Mothers, monastics and mystics of the Middle Ages; throughout the post-Reformation era; and continuing to the present time. Although the roots reach back into church history, a renewed interest in this prayer practice as an active Christian discipline has been growing over approximately the last sixty years. This growth is being influenced by the writings of Thomas Merton,[2] Thomas Keating,[3] Cynthia Bourgeault, John Main,[4] and the support of international Christian Contemplative Prayer networks such as

[2] Thomas Merton (1915–1968) has been noted as a very prominent American Catholic author. He has written many books including those related to monastic spirituality.

[3] Thomas Keating (1923–2018) was a founding member and spiritual leader of Contemplative Outreach, which serves to promote the development and growth of Christian Contemplative Prayer known as Centering Prayer.

[4] John Main (1926–1982) was the founding member and spiritual leader of the World Community for Christian meditation.

Contemplative Outreach[5] and the World Community for Christian Meditation.[6]

Many people from a variety of Christian faith traditions, backgrounds, and ethnicities are gradually becoming aware of the tradition of Christian Contemplative Prayer as a spiritual, quieting practice in a fast-paced world. However, despite the increased interest in this ancient prayer practice, research is limited in its investigation of the influence of Christian Contemplative Prayer in the lived experience of its practitioners.

Studies have investigated Eastern meditative practices, which can focus on self-awareness or self-actualization, yet less attention has been given to forms of Christian meditative, contemplative prayer. A few studies have investigated Christian Contemplative Prayer as an adjunct to psychotherapy, while more recently, some empirical studies have examined psychospiritual outcomes related to well-being. As this ancient prayer practice is growing within the Christian community, academic interest and understanding are advancing, yet many questions remain unanswered about this contemplative, spiritual path. The aim of the research study, on which this book is based, was to address the lacuna within published research examining the lived experience of long-term Christian Contemplative Prayer practitioners.

---

[5] 'Contemplative Outreach is a spiritual network of individuals and small faith communities committed to living the contemplative dimension of the Gospel. The common desire for Divine transformation, primarily expressed through a commitment to a daily Centering Prayer practice, unites our international, interdenominational community'. http://www.contemplativeoutreach.org/

[6] This international organization supports the practice of Christian Contemplative Prayer. Headquartered in London, England, and now at Bonnevaux in France, it nurtures individuals, and weekly groups as it promotes peace and compassion as 'spiritual fruits of meditation'. https://www.wccm.org/content/about-worldcommunity-christian-meditation

Defining Terms

Distinctions made between the terms 'meditation' and 'contemplation' are not always clear. Some have suggested that contemplation had a specific meaning during the early centuries of church history; however, more recently this word has developed other interpretations and meanings. Over time, or within different cultural and religious groups, the meaning or use of a word can change. The meaning of the word 'contemplation' has undergone striking changes in response to historical and cultural influences. We can be left questioning what contemplation and contemplative prayer are, and how they differ from meditation.

The word 'contemplation' is not entered in the multivolume *Encyclopedia of Religion* that was edited in the 1980s. Instead, one is referred to related entries such as meditation, prayer, silence, and attention. Similarly, the *Harper Collins Dictionary of Religion* provides an entry on meditation as: 'A process of contemplation usually undertaken in a structured manner'. John Main suggested that in the Christian context of meditation, he used the term meditation 'synonymously with such terms as contemplation, contemplative prayer, meditative prayer, and so on'.[7] Others have also referred to 'intentional silence' as it relates to contemplative prayer. These examples help to demonstrate that sometimes leaders and other writers do not make a distinction between contemplation and meditation. However, when Christians distinguish contemplation from meditation, contemplation is often characterized by a pause or rest from mental concentration, coupled with a simple awareness of

---

[7] John Main (2006) *Word into Silence*. Edited by Freeman, Laurence. Norwich: Canterbury Press.

being present with one's inner experience of God. This reflects the classical contemplative encounter with God of interior silence, as described in the sixteenth century by Saint John of the Cross.

This interchanging use of contemplation, contemplative prayer, and meditation can sometimes create confusion around the potential differences and similarities related to these terms. For the sake of clarity in this book, a distinction is made as to what defines contemplation and contemplative prayer, and how they are related to meditation.

Meditation – A practice of focusing the mind in reflection through the use of various concentrative, awareness, and receptive methods.

Christian Contemplative Prayer – A particular receptive form of meditation whereby, in silence, one lovingly gives their full attention or intention to God, passively releasing all other thoughts, thus leading one towards Christian contemplation in union with God.

Christian Contemplation – A silent, inactive state in which one's spirit rests quietly in union and openness to the indwelling Holy Spirit (presence) of God.

Additionally, there can be confusion surrounding the definition of two other important concepts which emerged in this research: well-being and embodiment. Within the context of this study, they are defined in the following ways:

Well-Being – A positive embodied state related to personal, social, environmental, and spiritual holistic health, as one becomes more aware and accepting of their own true self within social, environmental, and spiritual relationships. One's sense of well-being enhances one's connection with others, the environment, and God, helping to develop a greater sense of meaning, purpose, and God's presence.

Embodiment – One's embodied self (holistic human being: body, mind, and spirit) as integrated, contingent upon, and interacting with others and one's environmental space in an all-inclusive way, and in the case of Christian Contemplative Prayer, the embodied self as embodied in God completely.

Embodiment is further defined as the state of an individual that is conditional on the environment and the context of one's body. Therefore, an embodied individual (body, mind, and spirit) as an integral part of their environment contrasts with simply existing within one's surroundings. For example, one could live in a neighbourhood, that is, one could reside in that space and not even know their neighbours or anything else about that locale. Alternatively, one's holistic self could be embodied in their neighbourhood in such a way that integrates the whole person in relationships with their neighbours and interactively engages them within that environment. It is this inclusive expression of integration, wholeness, and embodiment that emerged as a foundational component of Christian Contemplative Prayer.

Conclusion

This research helps to advance our understanding of holistic well-being and the importance of embodiment within the spiritual discipline of Christian Contemplative Prayer. In embodied spiritual practices, the body is not excluded from our spirituality; however, we are at risk of idolatry if we place the body, rather than God, at the centre of our spiritual lives. Paul says: 'Glorify God in your body' (I Cor. 6:20). He does not say: 'Glorify your body.' Christian Contemplative Prayer enhances holistic well-being and engages one's whole being – body, mind, and spirit – in an embodied awareness of God's presence – *Glorifying God with body, mind, and spirit.*

2. Situating this Study

Christian Spirituality: A Multi-Disciplinary Academic Discipline

This chapter situates the study within the academic discipline of Christian Spirituality and in the historical developmental context of Christian Contemplative Prayer. Christian Spirituality pertains to experience, yet it is a term that can be difficult to define. Increasingly, laity, ministers, and scholars are interested in explorations of Christian Spirituality, which lie in the realm of lived experience within the Christian faith. This lived experience stems from a personal relationship with God, born out of a transformative, interactive communion with God. It is also recognized in the diversity of its spiritual practices. Within these differing practices, one experiences the unique ways in which God through the Holy Spirit reveals truth, communicates, guides, and makes His presence known to believers.

Within the Christian's spiritual lived experience is also a conscious process and a purposive involvement in their holistic spiritual growth. This holistic pursuit further supports a self-transcendence towards God. This self-transcendence is not the work of the individual, but rather that of the Holy Spirit bringing greater revelation of the triune God in the whole of one's life. Within the Holy Spirit's work of Christians' self-transcendence towards God there is a continued formation as spiritual beings in the image of Jesus. This is the lived experience of spirituality in the Christian's life.

Guided by the Holy Spirit, an individual's spirituality and practices can emerge in ways analogous to the development of their unique personality. Therefore, the spiritual experiences of Christians may vary, even within the same or different denominations, religious organizations, or movements. An important aspect of Christian Spirituality is the diversity of its spiritual practices; a diversification which also emerged in this study within the variability of Christian Contemplative Prayer practices. Additionally, spirituality is a process of integrating life holistically, through one's body, mind, and spirit, which involves an individual personally, socially, and environmentally in their interaction with God. One's Christian Contemplative Prayer practice was often seen as part of an integrated process to live more contemplatively, in ways that encompassed one's whole being.

Historical Survey of Christian Contemplative Prayer

During the first sixteen centuries of church history, contemplation appeared to be more common among devout clergy and lay people, after which time it appeared to wane. Then, beginning in the mid-twentieth century, interest in Christian spirituality and contemplation began to gain renewed importance. Although there has not been a specific method of Christian Contemplative Prayer until more recently, the contemplative themes of silence and stillness are seen within both the Old and New Testament Scripture and Christian church history.

Old Testament

Meditative references are found in the Psalms:

- 'Be still before the Lord and wait patiently for him...' (Psalm 37:7)
- 'Be still and know that I am God...' (Psalm 46:10)

These verses suggest a contemplative awareness, without directives on how to 'be still'.

New Testament Gospels

The basis of Christian Contemplative Prayer has continued to develop out of the practices and teachings of Jesus up through the present times. The exact way that Jesus prayed when He was alone is not clear, nor can one make a direct assertion to Christian Contemplative Prayer. It would be easier if we could recognize the exact ways that Jesus prayed when He was alone with God – ways that are supported by Scripture – but we simply can't. Jesus showed the necessity of solitude and prayer as He lived with a keen awareness of His union with God the Father. While His specific prayer methods are unclear, the importance of this focus in His life is undeniable.

Jesus' Teachings

Aspects of Christian Contemplative Prayer can also be recognized in Jesus' references and teachings, such as His recognition of God as Abba (Mark 14:36), His teachings on praying in secret (Matthew 6:6), and the description of 'the divine indwelling' (John 17:21–23a) in the Gospel of John. In Jesus' teaching on prayer in Matthew 6:6, He emphasized that true prayer is offered in secret. He states: 'But when you pray, go into your room, close the door and pray to your Father, who is unseen' (Matthew 6:6). This Scripture has been noted in various teachings on contemplation, from the fifth century John Cassian, through to the present teachings. Taken metaphorically, the reference to 'go into your room' is similarly acknowledged by the Desert Fathers and Mothers as the 'cave of your heart' and in this way, it creates a sense of closing the door to ordinary awareness. Jesus' lifestyle practice of retreating to quiet, secluded places, apart from the crowds where He could spend time in prayer with His Father, also exemplified this contemplative dimension:

- 'He went up on a mountainside by himself to pray.' (Matthew 14:23)
- 'And went off to a solitary place, where he prayed.' (Mark 1:35)
- 'He went up on a mountainside to pray.' (Mark 6:46)
- 'But Jesus often withdrew to lonely places and prayed.' (Luke 5:16)
- 'Jesus went out to a mountainside to pray, and spent the night praying to God.' (Luke 6:12)

For Jesus, the place of union with His Father is affirmed (John 10:30), further lending itself to that of contemplation. Some have identified a theological relation between Christian Contemplative Prayer and the biblical concept of kenosis ('to let go' or 'to empty oneself' in Greek). This concept describes the very nature of Christ, who emptied Himself to become human, and again when in the Garden of Gethsemane Jesus turned His will over to God.

New Testament Epistles

In the following excerpts from New Testament prayers, Paul encourages Christians to allow the work and presence of the Holy Spirit. He writes:

- 'I keep asking that the God of our Lord Jesus Christ, the glorious Father, may give you the Spirit of wisdom and revelation, so that you may know him better. I pray that the eyes of your heart may be enlightened...' (Ephesians 1:17–18a).
- 'I pray that out of his glorious riches he may strengthen you with power through his Spirit in your inner being...' (Ephesians 3:16).

In contemplative prayer, the Christian is obediently responding to the indwelling Spirit, which resonates with Paul's prayer for the believers. These prayers speak to the necessity for the Christian to understand what it means to open to Christ, as Christ is in the believer through the Holy Spirit (1 Corinthians 6:19; 2 Timothy 1:14). These understandings among Christian Contemplative Prayer practitioners reflect the roots of this Christian practice reaching back through time, into the Old Testament and New Testament teachings. These teachings are further reflected in the lives of the Desert Fathers and Mothers, who contemplatively sought the silence and solitude of the desert to seek after God.

Contemplative Prayer and the Desert Fathers and Mothers

During the third century, within the Roman Empire, many Christians were being persecuted. This served as a catalyst for some Christians to flee to the Egyptian desert and devote themselves to living their biblical ideals. Many of them became known as the Desert Fathers and Mothers. Then, in the fourth century, the prohibited cult of Christianity found itself thrust into the place of an imperial religion, again encouraging some to seek the truer expression of their faith by following the footsteps of Jesus into a more solitary, desert place. Consequently, from the third through to the sixth century, in the desert lands of Arabia, Egypt, Palestine, and Syria, a contemplative spirituality was growing. Through this, some found themselves led into the solitary practices of prayer life that they found in the desert, and towards the development of a more intentional awareness of God's presence. These Desert Fathers and Mothers incorporated the Psalms, the Scriptures, and a contemplative dimension into their life and prayers, which helped to support a growing tradition of Christian Contemplative Prayer.

Through these ascetic faithful devotees, the teachings of Christian Contemplative Prayer were further developed and integrated within the monastic movement. Of these, Abba Antony (c.251–356), also known as Saint Anthony the Great, was an important figure in the early growth of monasticism. He denied himself all that is of the world, fought with demons, and lived in solitude all for the sake of knowing God. He helped to establish a pattern of the contemplative life, setting the way not only for monasticism to be built but for the roots of contemplation to be nourished and developed. Evagrius Ponticus (c.345–399) was also among the Desert Fathers who practised a contemplative form of prayer as he believed that prayer should continue towards contemplation: a prayer without words. He recognized, however, that this form of prayer was clouded with the distraction of one's own thoughts. Evagrius was keenly aware of this struggle and dealing with these random thoughts became a focus in his developing contemplative method. He suggested meeting thoughts in prayer with simple awareness rather than with mental dialogue. Amma Sarah, as a Desert Mother, also worked to release the thoughts that might distract her focus on God in the purity of her heart. These early contemplatives of the Egyptian desert recognized the distracting mental activity and its disruption to their inner state of peaceful prayer. Similarly, although not considered one of the early Desert Fathers, Saint Augustine (c.354–430) insisted that after seasons of contemplative prayer and focusing one's prayerful attention away from these restless thoughts, one realizes the fruits of this stillness and inner focus that leads towards contemplation and greater awareness of union with God.

During the fourth and fifth centuries, John Cassian (c.360–435), a monk who founded two monasteries in France, wrote *Institutes* and *Conferences*. Cassian's *Conferences* were developed from his interviews with other desert monks and gave direction to silent, private prayer by insisting:

> *We need to be especially careful to follow the Gospel precept which instructs us to go into our [inner] room and shut the door so that we may pray to our Father. And this is how we can do it. We pray with the door shut whenever we withdraw our hearts completely from the tumult and noise of our thoughts and our worries and when secretly and intimately we offer our prayers to the Lord. We pray with the door shut when, without opening our mouths, and in perfect silence, we offer our petitions to the one who pays no attention to words but looks hard at our hearts.*

Cassian's practice and teachings later helped guide the development and practice of Centering Prayer (Appendix 1). Benedict of Nursia (c.480–547), often known as Saint Benedict, was influenced by the teachings of John Cassian, and is considered the father of Western monasticism. He was the founder of the Benedictine monastery, and his way of living and praying guided monastic living throughout Europe and became known as 'The Rule'. He also promoted the use of the phrase *lectio divina* as he focused on developing instructions for his monastic community and worked to build a rhythm of living that included intentional, contemplative attention on the reading of the Scripture. *Lectio divina* continued to develop in the monastic environment and became a method of prayerful listening to the Scripture, which could lead one into contemplation.

During the following century, Saint Gregory the Great (c.540–604) defined *contemplatio* as 'resting in God' because it was here that all faculties were quietly aware of the presence of God. For Saint Gregory, contemplation was not only a result of reflecting on the Scripture but was a gift and an experience of God, accessible to all Christians. As a monk, he experienced contemplation and union with God, yet he also struggled to balance his desire for the contemplative life with his acquired papal position of action. However, he believed these two aspects of contemplation and action should be integrated within one's inner and outer life, and in this way, they can complement one another.

Desert Fathers and Mothers continued the growth of Christian Contemplative Prayer, and although they were often isolated without any written Scripture and possibly even illiterate, their passion was to seek God. How these Desert Fathers and Mothers prayed is not clear; however, their total abandon of the world, enveloped in the silence and solitude of the desert wasteland, had a profound impact on many who would follow their teachings and practices throughout the Middle Ages.

Contemplative Prayer in the Middle Ages

Contemplation and prayer continued to be emphasized throughout the Middle Ages without any specific method. For medieval theologians, contemplation was biblical, and therefore it was practised and gained a stronger presence within monasticism. The stillness of the cloisters and monasteries had a symbolic significance, which helped to illustrate the eternal silence of God. In this way, they were a supportive space for contemplation. These monastics, spiritual teachers, and exemplars, both men and women, have remained a part of the foundation of contemporary Christian Contemplative Prayer practices.

One such leader, Saint Bernard of Clairvaux (c.1090–1153), was often recognized by many to be a master of the spiritual life and a monastic pillar of contemplation. He became known for encouraging a turning of the attention inward, as he embodied the spirituality of the Middle Ages. Saint Bernard recognized the scriptural reference of 2 Corinthians 3:18[8] as giving a contemplative perspective of the Spirit's transformative work within the Christian – towards the image of Christ.

During the twelfth century, Guigo the Carthusian (c.1114–1193) documented the method of *lectio divina* that had been informally

[8] 'And we all, who with unveiled faces contemplate the Lord's glory, are being transformed into his image with ever-increasing glory, which comes from the Lord, who is the Spirit' (2 Corinthians 3:18).

practised for centuries. He emphasized the components as a repetitive, slow reading of the scriptural text (*lectio*); meditating on the text (*meditatio*); praying from the text (*oratio*); and contemplating the text (*contemplatio*). *Lectio divina* is recognized by some as the classical way of nurturing contemplative prayer. While contemplation can appear to be the end of *lectio divina*, it can also be recognized as the beginning of learning that words are inadequate to express the sense of divine presence. At this point, one realizes a deeper communication with God. Guigo the Carthusian further described three levels of prayer. First, there were words; secondly, meditation on Scripture, as in *lectio divina*; and finally, Christian Contemplative Prayer which involved neither words nor ideas but an awareness of God's presence and resting in that presence.

An influential Franciscan friar, Bonaventure of Bagnoregio (c.1217–1274), is noted for his ability to balance the awareness of mystical communion and contemplation. 'Bonaventure's deeply incarnational spirituality is "user friendly" to a world that struggles to respect our bodies and the material world, and to a church that needs to be reminded of the Spirit's presence in every atom and molecule'.[9]

Two other spiritual leaders were Meister Eckhart (c.1260–1327) and Catherine of Genoa (c.1447–1510) whose ideas were reflected in *My deepest me is God*, a phrase representing the mystic sense of being present in prayer yet also being aware of another consciousness deeper than one's own. In this way, they were so present in contemplation that it felt they were a part of another consciousness and it was a part of them. This was their union with God.

---

[9] Dreyer 2007:176.

Contemplation and contemplative prayer continued to be illuminated in the lives of such great theologians as Julian of Norwich (c.1342–1420). She lived with a radical commitment to solitude, as reflected in her writings. While some lived solitary lives of contemplation, others such as Catherine of Sienna (c.1347–1380) exemplified a fusion of contemplation and action within their leadership and public life.

In the latter half of the fourteenth century, an anonymous treatise further depicted contemplative prayer – *The Cloud of Unknowing.* It was obscured until growing interest in spirituality brought increasing awareness to this way of Christian Contemplative Prayer. Little is known about the author except that he was a cloistered monk devoted to the contemplative life. Presenting a classical writing of the apophatic method of prayer, the author encouraged readers to release all thoughts, even those related to God. Although such thinking about God is still of value, it is not the work of apophatic prayer. The author's primary concern was 'with the art of contemplative prayer; "blind intent stretching to God" which, if it be wholly set on Him, cannot fail to reach its goal'.[10] The important contribution of this work to Christian Contemplative Prayer is its presentation of the mystical ascent to God, who cannot be fully understood and is shrouded in a cloud of mystery.

Monasticism and a contemplative way of prayer continued to grow as many Christian orders – including the Jesuits, Discalced Carmelites, Franciscans, Benedictines, and Trappists – placed a special importance on the practice of Christian Contemplative Prayer. Throughout the Middle Ages, contemplation was part of the ascetics'

---

[10] Anon. 2017:9.

discipline, and it remained an important part of one's realization of God's presence. The monastics dedicated a portion of their day to spiritual readings, prayer, and meditation. However, as the impact of the Reformation grew, monasticism struggled, and this diminished the practice of Christian Contemplative Prayer within the spiritual disciplines. Despite the pressures of the Reformation, Scholasticism, the Inquisition, and other Protestant shifts, Christian Contemplative Prayer and related practices continued.

Post-Reformation Contemplative Prayer

Thirteenth century Western Europe witnessed the rise of Scholasticism, with a progressive shift towards the intellect and away from experiential spirituality. During the Reformation, many European countries also saw a repression of monasteries. Many monastics were impacted by the Inquisition's heightened prosecution of Christians and the Inquisition's suspicion of the practice of silent prayer. The Protestant Reformation's emphasis on the reading of Scripture, preaching the Word, and church doctrine contributed to the marginalization of contemplative practices and apophatic prayer in the monastic tradition. Despite this resistance, contemplative spirituality continued to hold, and some of these faithful ascetics left an enduring influence on the contemplative tradition.

During this time, Saint John of the Cross' (c.1542–1591) *Dark Night of the Soul* helped depict the soul's journey towards union with God. Saint John of the Cross encouraged a contemplative approach in lovingly turning to God and embracing God in one's innermost being. Brother Lawrence (c.1611–1691) also portrayed the soul's journey towards union with God in his book – *The Practice of the Presence of God.* He admitted that the path to this perfect union was not easy, as he spent years disciplining his heart and mind to yield to God's presence.

In summary of the ensuing eighteenth and nineteenth centuries, Abbot Cuthbert Butler[11], in his book *Western Mysticism,* sums up the generally accepted view that had developed:

> *During the eighteenth and nineteenth centuries the idea had come to be accepted as well established, that, apart from special and unusual calls, the normal mental prayer for all was systematic discoursive meditation according to fixed method: this was taken to be the lifelong exercise of mental prayer for those embarked on a spiritual life – priests, religious, nuns, devout layfolk. Contemplation was looked on as something extraordinary, almost identified with visions, revelations, raptures, even stigmatization and levitation, and other such psycho-physical phenomena. Thus, contemplation and mystical theology had come to be regarded as wonderful, even miraculous; to be admired from a safe distance and left alone as dangerous and full of pitfalls. Such was the common view, such the common practice, almost taken for granted at the end of the nineteenth century.*

Post-Reformation teaching was opposed to earlier monastic traditions, and those who would even seek a contemplative form of prayer were considered in the realm of the miraculous, dangerous,

---

[11] 2011:x.

and even arrogant. This practice and its cautious acceptance remained through the end of the nineteenth century, yet contemplation continued to be practised because it was a theological, spiritual reality. During the twentieth century, there began to be renewed interest in contemplative prayer. This was attributed in part to studies regarding the history and theology of the ancient masters of spiritual life. Subsequently, interest in contemplative spirituality has been increasing over the past several decades, in conjunction with an increasing number of books related to this topic, and the development of international networks which support Christian Contemplative Prayer.

Modern Contemplative Prayer Practices in the Twentieth and Twenty-First Centuries

During the latter half of the twentieth century, several authors helped to foster a renewed interest in this spiritual practice. They recognized the contemplative aspect of prayer, which had become merely a reflection of an important part of Christian spirituality from the past. In 1964, Merton published a book titled *The Wisdom of the Desert*, which helped to reveal foundational insights into this ancient experience and practice. In his twenty-first century essay, 'Three Contemplative Waves', David Frenette, a leader and senior teacher in the Centering Prayer movement, argued that God is again bringing about 'a living witness to the contemplative dimension of the Gospel' just as He did with the Desert Fathers and Mothers.[12] Frenette saw this divine work progressing in the nature of three waves, just as in nature each ocean wave is formed from the waters of the previous

[12] 2008:13.

wave, but in a new way. This momentum is further developing a growing international network of Christian Contemplative Prayer practitioners.

First Wave of Contemplative Prayer: Thomas Merton (1915–1968)

Merton's writings on contemplation grew and evolved as the momentum for the 'first wave' of renewal in Christian Contemplative Prayer. The life of Merton became a surrender to seeking God through the apophatic method of prayer. His writings included topics related both to contemplative Christianity and the spiritual exemplars of the past. The essence of Merton's work served to bring contemplation actively into the realm of Christian spirituality again. This accentuated the need to promote contemplative practices outside of the monasteries. The next wave of Christian Contemplative Prayer expansion helped to bring these aspects into clearer focus and served to guide non-monastic Christians into contemplative prayer and its practice. Solitude, silence, simplicity, and a discipline for prayer and action can be supported within the environment of the monastery; however, they are increasingly difficult to maintain in the world outside that community. The second wave has enabled the necessary support and a framework for practising Christian Contemplative Prayer within a broader Christian community.

Second Wave of Contemplative Prayer: Thomas Keating (1923–2018) and John Main (1926–1982)

In the 1970s, a 'second wave' followed with the development of Centering Prayer as Keating and other theologians worked to simplify the apophatic method of prayer found in the medieval mystical classic *The Cloud of Unknowing*. They condensed the book's seventy-five chapters into three basic steps or rules, proposing an abridged approach to Christian Contemplative Prayer. This method was called Centering Prayer. It helped to represent the classical contemplative experience of interior silence described by Saint John of the Cross in the sixteenth century. Its name also kept with Merton's use of the word 'center' as the place of the contemplative encounter with God. In this way, the Centering Prayer method helped to further promote the development of contemplative prayer within the Christian tradition.

With this second wave, the practice of Christian Contemplative Prayer continued to grow, and its momentum was further supported by the organization of Contemplative Outreach. Formed shortly after the first intensive Centering Prayer retreat in 1983, this has become a community support system for practitioners as it has served to enhance the global growth of Christian Contemplative Prayer. This organization aids in the dispersion of written, audio, and video material related to the practice of Centering Prayer, fostering local and global networks of Christian practitioners and a renewal of the contemplative dimension of Christianity.

Another important second wave influencer was John Main, who became a Benedictine monk in 1958. In his studies of John Cassian and the Desert Fathers and Mothers, he discovered the way of Christian Contemplative Prayer, which he began to practice. In 1975, at Ealing Abbey in London, he founded the first Christian Meditation Centre. He taught the discipline of practicing his simple form of prayer, which he believed could lead people to a deeper spiritual experience as a prayer of the heart. He was invited in 1977 by the Archbishop of Montreal, Paul Grégoire, to establish a Benedictine Priory committed intentionally to the practice and teaching of Christian meditation. The World Community for Christian Meditation grew out of his work and was established after his death by Laurence Freeman and the community of Christian meditation groups that were touched by John Main's teachings. For Main, prayer was not just talking to God or thinking about Him, but it was about being present with the divine. He taught that through silence, stillness, and simplicity, one's relationship with God can be deepened.

Third Wave of Contemplative Prayer: Ammas and Abbas Outside the Monasteries

There are hints of a 'third wave' of renewal driven by the Ammas and Abbas, whom some recognize as the animators of the contemplative life. These Ammas and Abbas are living their lives outside the monastery, integrated within a contemplative lifestyle, and they can serve as the teachers and spiritual mothers and fathers for those wishing to develop a contemplative spirituality. The full development of this potential third wave is yet to be seen; however, many of those involved in the development of Christian Contemplative Prayer practices contend that it is incarnational – the work of the divine within humanity.

Conclusion

This chapter has outlined the academic discipline of Christian Spirituality, which has functioned as a hermeneutical scaffolding supporting this study. This chapter has also given a brief survey of the history and development of Christian Contemplative Prayer practice and its related themes of solitude and silence, which are recognized throughout the teachings and practices found within Scripture and the history of the Christian church. Although some of the current Christian Contemplative Prayer approaches and methods may differ slightly, there is a commonality that connects these practices in their focus on the presence of God.

3. Literature Review

Christian Contemplative Prayer Scholarship

Although prayer is of central importance within religion, limited studies exist related to this spiritual practice. One such early comprehensive study was Heiler's (1932) phenomenological investigation of prayer, in which he identifies mystical prayer as seeking union with God and practised as a silent attentiveness to God rather than verbal communication. Heiler believed that mystical prayer was incompatible with Christianity, which is an argument that has been debated by scholars. This challenging debate is supported by some theologians who recognize that both verbal and silent prayers are still the work of the Holy Spirit as in Romans 8:15–16.[13] Verbal prayer is recognized within such categories as adoration, petitioning, thanksgiving, and intercession. However, mystical prayer is associated with Christian Contemplative Prayer and can be recognized as giving one's full attention to God's presence. Christian Contemplative Prayer can further be realized as a waiting on God as one's confidence in God's power and love deepens.

[13] Romans 8:15–16 '… The Spirit himself testifies with our spirit that we are God's children'.

Some researchers have investigated the benefits of Christian Contemplative Prayer as an adjunct to psychotherapy, finding limited circumstantial evidence of this prayer's complementary usefulness to psychotherapy. However, researchers realize that prayer also presents difficulties in quantitative studies, and one cannot fully account for the working of the Holy Spirit in an individual.

Other studies have investigated the lived experience of Centering Prayer practitioners. They found that the experience and increased awareness of God through Centering Prayer was multidimensional. They noted decreases in anxiety and stress, as practitioners also experienced themselves as less judgemental, more compassionate, and increasingly accepting of themselves. These studies suggested that Centering Prayer helps the practitioner to move forward even during times of spiritual dryness, helping them to increase their depth of faith in God.

A few studies have found that Centering Prayer sometimes brings to the surface difficult emotions, memories, images, or other psychological material that has been repressed. However, they found that the reintegration of these suppressions did not coincide with declines in mental health. This suggests that Centering Prayer may prevent the pathological affect that religious crisis can create. Although there are limitations in many of these studies, they all suggest that Centering Prayer is an effective practice for reducing anxiety in individuals.

Early streams of research described Christian Contemplative Prayer as waiting on God in a passive, non-demanding, and non-verbal way, where one's experience and concept of God changed from being a distant and remote figure to an intimate presence within. This exemplifies the Scripture, 'It is now no longer I that live but Christ lives in me' found in Galatians 2:20. Continued research efforts have added to our limited understanding of Christian Contemplative Prayer and its influence on the practitioner; however, endeavours in empirical studies with carefully planned research designs continue to be warranted.

Well-Being

According to the United States Center for Disease Control: 'Well-being is a positive outcome that is meaningful for people and for many sectors of society, because it tells us that people perceive that their lives are going well'. Researchers have recognized two general well-being perspectives: hedonic and eudaemonic. Hedonic well-being is recognized in terms of seeking pleasure or happiness and avoiding pain; however, this perspective does recognize that some pleasure-producing outcomes are not good for people. Eudaemonic well-being, on the other hand, promotes the realization of one's potential, and the recognition of one's true self that leads to a meaningful life. While a hedonic assessment tends towards experiences, eudaemonic relies more on the fully functioning individual.

The contrast between these two philosophies of hedonic and eudaemonic has provoked much debate as to the best ways to measure well-being, although assessing well-being has become important within various disciplines, including psychology and spirituality. This further supports the need for precision in one's definition of well-being and the importance of a holistic approach. The concept of defining well-being solely as happiness has been questioned by scholars, who have advocated the importance of defining well-being in terms of 'optimal psychological functioning'. These varying descriptions of well-being have generated diverse investigations regarding causes, consequences, and aspects of well-being. Studies that only include eudaemonic measures leave out hedonic indicators of the pleasures of life. Additionally, until recently, psychology has focused on pathology and the treatment of mental illness more than on health or well-being; however, in the last few decades that has changed.

There is also a growing interest in studying spiritual well-being as it relates to health promotion, yet there are a minimal number of well-validated research instruments to measure aspects of spiritual well-being and spirituality. This presents some difficulties not only in defining spirituality, but also assessing the spiritual well-being of an individual. In 1999, well-being and education scholar John Fisher developed a spirituality instrument, the Spiritual Health and Life-Orientation Measure (SHALOM), that assesses four domains related to spiritual well-being (Table 1).

Table 1 SHALOM Four Domains

Personal	**Communal**
Sense of identity Self-awareness Joy in life Inner peace Meaning in life	Love of other people Forgiveness towards others Trust between individuals Respect for others Kindness towards other people
Environmental	**Transcendental**
Connection with nature Awe at a breath-taking view Oneness with nature Harmony with the environment Sense of 'magic' in the environment	Personal relationship with the divine/God Worship of the Creator Oneness with God Peace with God Prayer life

(Fisher 2010:109)

This is a useful tool to measure spiritual well-being, as it includes various aspects of one's embodied being. Despite the complications surrounding the analysis of well-being, studies continue within varying disciplines amidst differing well-being definitions. This study aims to present a multidimensional approach to body, mind, and spirit well-being.

Embodiment

Along with well-being, embodiment became a central theme within this investigation of Christian Contemplative Prayer. Christian theology integrates the body, mind, and spirit, especially in the teachings of the creation of humankind, the Incarnation, the Christian as the temple of God, and the Body of Christ. This section further discusses the interrelation of embodiment within the lived experience of Christian Contemplative Prayer, as the harmonious, whole person is integrated and influenced within this prayer practice.

Since the 1980s, conceptual understandings of embodiment have developed from studies which have helped to advance these more holistic ideas, integrating the body, and reflecting upon an individual's actions being centred in one's physical body. This has challenged the idea that the body's role is to supply input to the mind, which operates independently in the body as the sole processor of information. In the mid-1900s, French philosopher Maurice Merleau-Ponty espoused ideas related to embodiment to explain the interaction between the mind and the body. He recognized the Importance of the physical body's knowledge and awareness within its environment, and the subsequent influence the body enacted on the consciousness of the individual.

Embodiment can be further related to such aspects as historical, physical, and social embodiment (Table 2).

These perspectives reflect upon an individual's sense of knowing as it relates to their physical body and understanding within their environment.

Table 2 Examples of Perspectives on Embodiment

Historical Embodiment: **Effects of historical interactions within one's environment**
Social Embodiment: **Proceeding from one's social interactions within one's environment**
Physical Embodiment: **Relating to the physical body's sensorimotor connection within one's environment**

Ziemke 2013

Body/Mind/Spirit, Cartesian Dualism, and the Enlightenment's Influence

Although embodied cognition and related ideas might be difficult to define, concepts related to embodiment contrast with other dualistic characterizations of the rational processes of the mind and the subservient body. Rene Descartes' Cartesian dualism held that the mind was a non-physical and therefore non-spatial entity that was identified with the individual's consciousness and awareness. While distinguishing it from the brain as the centre of cognition, he recognized the mind's influence on the body. Throughout the Enlightenment, philosophical thought continued to promote mind–

body dualism, integrating ideas of separating mental thought from the physical body and noting the distinctness of the mind and the body. However, only recently has there been a greater understanding of the body's influence on cognition and the understanding of the self in its environment.

As the field of cognitive science has seen a shift towards more embodied views of the situated self in its environment, there have also been increasing developments in the understanding of the body in seated meditation and mindfulness. These studies bring attention to the important aspect of embodiment in meditation. Studies have further examined the influence of movement-based embodied contemplative practices while recognizing the connection of embodiment, integration of movement, and the interrelatedness within the contemplative practice.

Embodiment and Christianity

The Creation of Humankind

The idea of *imago Dei*, the image of God, integrates the body, mind, and spirit within the creation of human beings as it reflects on the totality of the individual. In the Book of the Psalms, the Psalmist recognizes their being as created by God: 'For you created my inmost being; you knit me together in my mother's womb. I praise you because I am fearfully and wonderfully made' (Psalm 139:13–14). The total created human being embodies a physical form through which all of life can be experienced.

The Incarnation

Theologians recognize the importance of the body as witnessed in the Incarnation of Christ, which exemplifies the profound confirmation of the sacredness of the physical world. As the Word became flesh and dwelt among humanity in the person of Jesus Christ, humankind become keenly aware of the interconnection of the indwelling spirit within the human body. This manifestation depicted the intimate relationship between God and humanity. God's revelation through the body of Jesus allowed a different perspective of intimacy with the divine, and in a sense, God became accessible in a physical form. The Incarnation is the perfect example of glorifying God in a physical body, reflecting the importance of one's body within one's spiritual disciplines.

The Embodied Self as the Temple of God

In this sense, humans relate with God in and through their bodies, even as Scripture declares: 'For God's temple is holy, and you are that temple' (1 Corinthians 3:17). Not only is the physical body one's holistic presence in the physical world but for the Christian the body is the indwelt sacred space of God's presence. The body can also be recognized as an important element of spiritual formation. Thus, embodiment is being further recognized within theological aspects of creation, the Incarnation, and the individual as the temple of God.

Conclusion

Even though research around Christian Contemplative Prayer practice is on the rise, there are still many unanswered questions.

This study provides insights into participants' understanding of their long-term Christian Contemplative Prayer practice, its lived experience, and its influence on their well-being in an embodied context. It is important to recognize that aspects of well-being and embodiment are not the only overarching themes within Christian Contemplative Prayer practice, but they are the specific focus of this research through its grounded theory investigation of this study's participants.

4. The Findings of this Study

This chapter describes, abstracts, and conceptualizes the grounded theory data emerging from the thirty-six participant interviews (Please see Appendix 2 for a brief quote from each participant). The following sections outline this research's emerging specific conceptual categories: *Christian Contemplative Prayer, Well-being,* and *Embodiment.* Each of these three conceptual categories is further characterized by the associated concepts, properties, and dimensions.

Conceptual Category – Christian Contemplative Prayer

The first main conceptual category is *Christian Contemplative Prayer,* which is delineated in the table overleaf. The concepts in Table 3 relate to the prayer practice itself, including participants' initial introduction to Christian Contemplative Prayer.

Discovery of Christian Contemplative Prayer

Some participants were drawn to silence and solitude at an early age. Then, as they continued to mature there was a natural transition to

Table 3 Conceptual Category – Christian Contemplative Prayer: Coding Structure

Conceptual Category	Concept	Property	Dimension
Christian Contemplative Prayer (CCP) (The practice)	Initial Introduction to CCP	Personal influence	• Drawn to silence • Dissatisfaction/seeking more • Reading CCP books
		Communal influence	• Invited by someone • Attend info meeting • Monasterial participation
	Beyond Words	Spectrum of understanding	• Understand some aspects • Incomprehensible mystery
		Defies simple description	• Inexplainable • Words can only point to it
	Silent Prayer	Personal silence and solitude	• Recognize the value of silence • Drawn to silence
		Communal silence	• Collective intention • Powerful
		Cultural contemplation	• CCP not always silent • Cultural/tradition variations
	CCP Methods	Various Methods	• Embodied Sitting • Embodied Movement
		Same Intention	• Contemplation in God • Union with God

incorporate this silent prayer practice into their spiritual discipline. Others found that as adults they noticed an increasing spiritual awareness of desperation or emptiness, causing them to seek out something more in their spiritual discipline, life, and relationship with God. Others were burnt out or simply seeking a deeper relationship with God.

For some, their own personal searching was the catalyst in their introduction to Christian Contemplative Prayer, while for others there was a communal association that helped to initiate their practice. This community influence sometimes came through a friend, religious leader, or even a counsellor. Others became exposed to Christian Contemplative Prayer through their participation in an informative group event, such as gatherings centred on *lectio divina*, or a group event possibly at a monastery, convent, or priory. As participants shared their discovery of and their experience within this spiritual discipline, there was often a profound realization that there are elements of this practice that go beyond words. This practice is focused on being with God – an experience itself that can go beyond description.

Silent Prayer

Through Christian Contemplative Prayer, God can be recognized 'in' the silence as a place to watch, wait, and become more aware of His presence. Yet, while silence could be appreciated alone with God, it could also be experienced within a group of Christian Contemplative Prayer practitioners. Some noted that the group prayer can help to ease the discomfort with silence that can sometimes be experienced within this practice. Frustration in silence could also be influenced by distracting environmental sounds. However, this practice is a process of focusing on God's presence, learning to sit in the silence, letting go of mental distractions, and being less encumbered by the silence itself or seemingly intruding, external noises.

Christian Contemplative Prayer Methods

Participants expressed that their Christian Contemplative Prayer practice was connected to a developing awareness of listening to

God more, instead of doing the usual talk, talk, talk. Yet, within this realization was the surprising variability of the actual methods. For many, Christian Contemplative Prayer began and ended in some form of a relaxed, often seated, open posture; however, some participant methods began to exhibit forms of movement or activity that seemed to help quiet individuals. Each of the varying methods moved one towards contemplation and awareness of union with God. In that silence, one was eventually resting in God's presence, releasing other thoughts and actions.

Within this recognition of various methods was the realization that people, their personalities, their Christian faith tradition, and personal perspectives can all vary and need to be recognized as an integral aspect of this practice. One participant summed up the thoughts of others with this comment:

> *I have come to realize that I cannot be so arrogant to know what someone's relationship with God should look like.*

In their affirmation of various methods of contemplative prayer leading to contemplation, participants described the following approaches within their prayer practice (Figure 1 opposite and Table 4 overleaf).

Participants delineated the specifics of these activities, relating them to individual Christian Contemplative Prayer practice, or to prayer practised in a group setting. The activities assisted in the process of settling the practitioner, releasing physical energy, and helping to quiet their being. Within one prayer time, these various Christian Contemplative Prayer methods often led to a cessation of the method, with the practitioner resting in silent contemplation with God.

Figure 1 Various Methods of Contemplative Prayer Leading to Contemplation

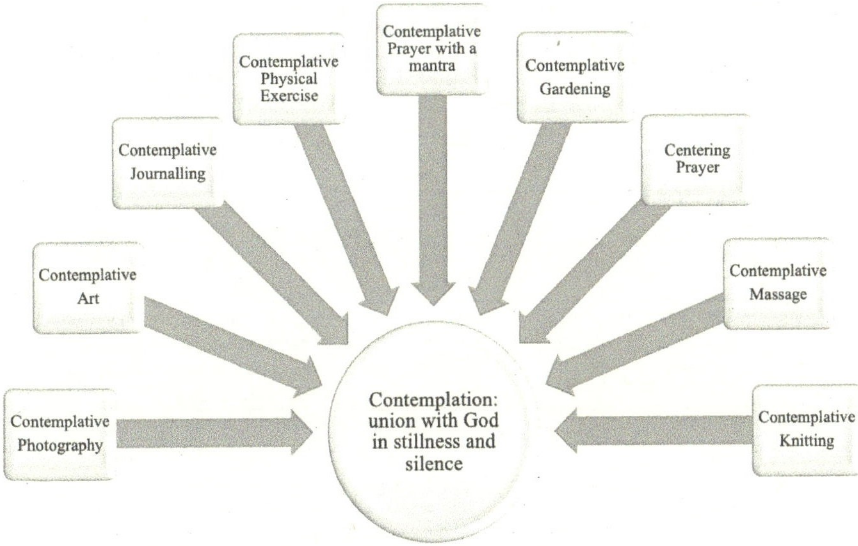

Yoga

A few practitioners spoke of yoga as an embodied physical exercise incorporated into their Christian Contemplative Prayer practice. They stated that their yoga was focused on movement and posture, which helped bring them to a place of stillness and rest in God's presence. For these practitioners, yoga itself was not the prayer practice but rather they saw it as merely postural and separated from any other religious and spiritual traditions. However, not all Christian Contemplative Prayer practitioners or Christians support the practice of yoga, as they feel it cannot be fully detangled from its spiritual and

Table 4 Examples of Methods of Embodied Christian Contemplative Prayer

Method	Method description - (individual or group)
Contemplative Photography	A silent walk while photographing, followed by a quiet contemplative gaze at the photos to receive in the photo something from God
Contemplative Art	Silent artistic time, including various artistic mediums
Contemplative Journalling	Silent journaling — Often includes journaling around any given topic, or really no topic at all
Contemplative Physical Exercise	Any variety of silent physical activities (e.g. Biking/Jogging/Walking)
Contemplative Prayer with mantra	Sitting in silence, with one's intention in God, and using a 'silent' mantra (e.g. 'Maranatha' or 'Jesus') to re-direct one's thoughts back to a present awareness of God's presence
Contemplative Gardening	Being present with God in the quiet garden
Centering Prayer	Silently, in stillness, centering one's intention on the experience of God's presence
Contemplative Massage	A time of being present with God, in silence and stillness, during massage
Contemplative Knitting	Knitting (keeping one's hands occupied), while releasing thoughts, and sitting in silence with one's intention focused on God

religious roots. They believe that not recognizing the spiritual intent of the yoga 'poses' does not transform them into merely postural bodily exercises without any potential for continuing spiritual consequences or influence on one's beliefs.

Conceptual Category – Well-Being

The second main conceptual category is *Well-Being*, which is delineated in the table overleaf. The concepts in Table 5 relate to the prayer practice and its influence on the various holistic concepts of well-being.

Personal Well-Being

Within the concept of Personal Well-Being participants realized a growing sense of peace, patience, and lessening anxiety in their lives. They described a greater self-awareness, and through that a process of becoming more authentic with both themselves and others. There was also a belief in healing through Christian Contemplative Prayer, recognized by some to be holistic, transformative, or even curative. Some also expressed a perception of healing within their memories or emotions, explaining that the memories don't go away, but they are healed. Participants' improving sense of well-being was also realized within their interpersonal or communal relationships, contributing to a fuller sense of both personal and communal embodied well-being.

Communal Well-Being

Communal well-being is reflected in a general sense of improving and restoring relationships. Improvement within relationships was also related to improvements in one's self, including a growing sense of knowing and loving one's self. The participants themselves found an increasing ability to be forgiving, accepting, patient, open, and peaceful, which was further enhanced by being generally less judgemental and less angry towards others. They also recognized a sense of growing in compassion and love for other people as they became more authentic within their relationships.

Table 5 Well-Being

Conceptual Category	Concept	Property	Dimension
Well-Being	Personal Well-Being	Meaning and core values	• Strengthening core values • Valuing developing core values
		Self-awareness	• Recognizing 'true self' • Becoming more of 'true self'
		Healing	• Ongoing process • Holistic
	Communal Well-Being	Others noticing the changes	• Valuing others' perception • Others complimenting changes
		Restoring relationships	• Resolving conflicts • Letting go of past hurts
		Improving relationships	• Accepting • Patient • Forgiving • Loving • More open • Less anger • Less judging • More authentic • Peaceful
	Environmental Well-Being	Effecting	• Effect the world
		Connecting	• Creating and connection to the Creator • More connected with creation
		Appreciating	• In nature • Creation's awe
	Spiritual Well-Being	Growing	• More spiritual
		Recognizing	• Realizing one's identity as a child of God • Recognizing God as loving
		Accepting	• Openness to God's presence • Allowing the Spirit to work

Environmental Well-Being

Environmental well-being was perceived in participants through a sense of Christian Contemplative Prayer's potential effect on the world and all of creation. Many believed that when they practised Christian Contemplative Prayer it went beyond just themselves, extending to all of humanity and all that God created. Additionally, a ripple effect was also recognized as a deeper sense of connection with all of creation. Ultimately, their sense of connection and embodiment within creation gave them a sense of greater connection with their Creator God. This interrelatedness with creation and nature also helped them to perceive nature with greater awe and see the power within nature for healing.

Spiritual Well-Being

Practitioners spoke about their spiritual well-being from the perspective of their relationship and awareness of God in their life. Through their long-term practice, Christian Contemplative Prayer helped to integrate an awareness of letting go and trusting God, which helped develop an increased opening for God's Spirit working in them and guiding their lives. As practitioners became more aware of God's presence in the moment, they also became more aware of God speaking into their lives and guiding their choices.

As they recognized God's acceptance and love for them in a deeper way, their relationship with Him grew and developed more thoroughly. In many cases, they found themselves identifying more as beloved children of God. These aspects gave them a sense of greater spiritual well-being, realizing that they did not have to earn God's love and that God accepts them for who they are. They became more aware of God's presence and love within their relationships and throughout their daily embodied lived experiences.

Conceptual Category – Embodiment

The third main conceptual category is *Embodiment*, which is delineated in the table below. The concepts in Table 6 relate to embodiment within this prayer practice, especially as embodied self, embodied in Christian community, embodied space, and embodied in God.

Embodied Self

The first concept within the conceptual category of Embodiment is *Embodied Self*. This emerged in participants' understanding of

Table 6 Embodiment

Conceptual Category	Concept	Property	Dimension
Embodiment	Embodied Self	Experienced in one's body	• Body awareness • Body knowledge • Body participation
		Anchored in the present	• Centring in one's body • In the present with I AM
		Connecting body, mind, and spirit	• Incarnation • Valuing embodiment
	Embodied in Christian Community	Support	• Easier to sit in silence together • Group Christian Contemplative Prayer can strengthen one's personal Christian Contemplative Prayer
		Collective intention	• More powerful • Being present
		Connected in love	• Importance of community • Love of others connected to love of self and God

Embodiment	Embodied Space	Empirical space	• Silent space • Relaxed space • Safe space • Peaceful space • Better space • Difficult space • Resting space • Wonderful space • Physical space • Simple/basic space • A space in nature • Familiar space
		Creating space	• Intentional space • Creating a 'tent' space • Holding a space for others
		Sacred space	• A space to commune with God • God as space • Contemplative space/Entering that meditative space • Receptive space • Communal space
	Embodied in God	Heightened awareness	• God's presence • God's patience • Being present with I AM
		Relationship with God	• Connection with God • Coming to God • Overflowing in God's love
		Contemplative union with God	• Temple of God within • God's embodiment: The Incarnation • Unceasing prayer • Contemplation

themselves as integrated, holistic, created human beings in body, mind, and spirit. In this way, embodiment was recognized as a very important aspect of long-term Christian Contemplative Prayer practitioners' lived experience. This begins to reflect the importance of embodiment, as some even recognized the passive role of their body in their prayer practice. They described themselves as often sitting upright in a seat, their feet flat on the ground, with hands and arms relaxed, or simply kneeling the entire time on a pad on the floor, in stillness and silence. Participants recognized how their body anchored them in the present – where God is. In this way, practitioners felt that their body kept them in the present, helping them not ruminate on the past or feel anxious about the future. While recognizing that God is timeless, they spoke of the name that God used in referencing Himself: 'I AM', as indicating God's presence in the present tense.

Embodied in Christian Community

The second concept within the conceptual category of Embodiment is *Embodied in Christian Community*. Within this concept was the recognition of the important role of one's Christian Contemplative Prayer community in one's personal prayer practice. In the group, there was a sense of community, connection, and belonging, with a realization as the Body of Christ in contemplative union together with God. There was a very profound recognition that the group Christian Contemplative Prayer was a more powerful, energizing experience, as one participant articulated, which helps one 'consent' to a deeper level within oneself. They also found that sitting quietly in Christian Contemplative Prayer often came easier within the group. Many participants recognized this difference within the group as being distinct, yet it was still very difficult to express what the difference was. Participants were also aware of a growing sense of love for not only those within their prayer group but also love and connection for other people, even as a spiritual sense of connection and caring for one another.

Embodied Space

The third concept within the conceptual category of Embodiment is *Embodied Space.* This concept reflects a space or place that could be physically, mentally, and spiritually embodied, and sensed in different ways. These various understandings of space are an intricate part of participants' lived experience of Christian Contemplative Prayer. Sometimes described as a space to let go, a safe space, a peaceful space, a transforming space, or a space in nature to be alone with God in silence. Sometimes participants spoke about creating space for themselves to be with God, while some group prayer leaders spoke of simply 'holding' that space for others.

Finally, a conceptual idea that seemed to permeate all aspects of the space was the importance of it being an understood space. The importance of being in a space in which one was comfortable, a space to be understood and release all to God, with a desire to create a space for God to reveal who He is, without the limitations of one's own expectations.

Embodied in God

The fourth concept within the conceptual category of Embodiment is *Embodied in God.* In their heightened consciousness of God's presence, this concept includes being able to open one's self more fully and more completely to God, helping participants to be more honest about perceived imperfections and become even more receptive to God's love for them. Through their openness with God and receiving God's love for them, practitioners' Christian Contemplative Prayer practice allowed them a place of rest for their whole being to be embodied in the presence of the triune God. They felt more connected to God through their contemplative union with Him.

As participants spoke about the importance of their holistic embodied self being centred in and through their bodies, they also affirmed the importance of the human body within the Incarnation. They highlighted the Incarnation of God in Christ as essential to their understanding of the value of not only the body, but the created value of the holistic embodied self as the temple of God's spiritual presence within. Their growing awareness of God's presence in their life also created a greater appreciation for unceasing prayer in their life. It was their growing consciousness of God's embodied triune presence in their Christian Contemplative Prayer practice that helped participants develop an increasing realization of God with them in communion throughout the day.

Conclusion

This chapter has summarised the data and resultant emerging conceptual categories, as nuanced by their concepts, properties, and dimensions. The following chapter will discuss these findings as the conceptual categories are informed by the Christian Contemplative Prayer literature in an integrated presentation of the lived experience of long-term Christian Contemplative Prayer practitioners.

5. Discussion

Christian Contemplative Prayer

The findings of this study continue to explore aspects of well-being and begin to develop the under-theorized concept of embodiment within Christian Contemplative Prayer. They also develop greater understanding of practitioners' initial attraction to this prayer form, the meanings found within this practice, and the different ways in which Christian Contemplative Prayer is practised. This continues to build upon the limited scholarship related to this prayer practice, especially in the lived experience of long-term practitioners.

Developing Christian Spirituality Depth

As the findings indicated, it was sometimes because of participants' own desperation, dissatisfaction, or desire for a deeper relationship with God that drew them towards Christian Contemplative Prayer. In this prayer practice, they found a spiritual discipline that helped them to develop a greater depth in their Christian spirituality. In this way, participants became more grounded in their spiritual journey towards greater awareness of the presence of God as developed through the power of the Holy Spirit and mediated by Jesus Christ. In God's presence, they found greater communion and union with God and all of creation. A relationship with God may reflect this goal of many Christians' spiritual lives and it is an integral aspect of Christian Contemplative Prayer.

Growing in Communal Christian Spirituality

The personal longing for more led some to connect to a Christian Contemplative Prayer practice through other Christians' invitations or teachings. This process often led participants to greater spiritual community development. As others were sought out who participated in this prayer practice, there developed a common bond in their desire for the divine's presence that further reinforced their interpersonal connections.

Prayer practitioners found that the spiritual community often transcends the individual and provides support for understanding spiritual experiences. Most importantly, a community outside of oneself may confront and encourage one to develop a deeper, fuller relationship with God. For many participants, their initial attraction to and integration of this group prayer practice also influenced greater embodied communal spirituality development.

Conscious Development of Christian Contemplative Prayer Practice

Christian spirituality is often part of one's conscious process of spiritual growth, and a conscientious effort was also noted in the ways that participants were drawn to and developed their long-term prayer practice. Some read books on spiritual growth and Christian Contemplative Prayer, and/or attended related workshops, conferences, and classes. There was also participation in silent retreats or even short-term residential lived experiences at monasteries and priories. Various participants gained spiritual direction in Christian Contemplative Prayer, while others sought Christian Contemplative Prayer counsel from friends or the broader Christian community. Some practitioners intentionally pursued involvement in this prayer practice, and consciously pursued a faithful, long-term Christian Contemplative Prayer practice.

At the World Community for Christian Meditation's monastery in Bonnevaux, there was a very consistent, punctual attentiveness to the daily communal Christian Contemplative Prayer practice for all transient and permanent residents. A bell rang routinely at three specific times during the day. All residents would disengage from their current activity and meet in the chapel for a time of Christian Contemplative Prayer. Outside the monastery environment, many recognized the complexities of life sometimes interfered with their desire to practice Christian Contemplative Prayer twice a day; however, for many this practice had become integral in their lives and had been practised consistently for many years. Furthermore, as noted in the findings, sometimes differing contemplative methods were discovered and practised.

Various Christian Contemplative Prayer Methods

The diversity among Christians and their various life stages exemplified the uniqueness of individual Christians' lived experience. This was a vital aspect of participants' expression of their Christian Contemplative Prayer practice. Various methods emphasized the importance of allowing and accepting uniqueness among Christian Contemplative Prayer practitioners, while recognising that these methods still brought practitioners to a place of silence and stillness within an intentional contemplation in union with God. The goal was the same, although it was reached by various paths. The uniquely personal aspects of this practice coupled with the aspects of well-being and transcendence were all foundational elements that brought recognition to Christian Contemplative Prayer as a consciously pursued and embodied spiritual practice.

Well-Being

Christian Contemplative Prayer Well-Being Mirrors Eudaemonia

Individuals came to their Christian Contemplative Prayer practice from their own experiences and disposition in life; therefore, their personal path to well-being was similar, yet unique to each individual. Participants expressed aspects of eudaemonic well-being related to wholeness, self-awareness, and meaning, all developing within their life as they continued their Christian Contemplative Prayer practice. This helped to bring participants a greater awareness of their interior life. These influences not only brought such progressive changes as an increased sense of peace, centredness, and authenticity, but also an ability to make different positive choices, with greater awareness of one's own emotions, acceptance of self, and healthier relationships with others.

Communal Well-Being

A comprehensive understanding of an individual's well-being extends beyond the individual to include the integration of interpersonal relationships. This is consistent with eudaemonic well-being. As participants became more aware of their true self, they also developed a greater authenticity in their interpersonal relationships. As they recognized greater peace within themselves, they found they were also better equipped to handle difficult emotional, interpersonal situations instead of merely reacting to them. These improved relationships helped participants to realize a more positive, integrated sense of eudaemonic well-being in relation to themselves, others, and the world around them.

Environmental Well-Being

Christian Spirituality also explores how divine relationship informs one's interaction with the environment, strengthening one's connection not only with God, but also deepening an appreciation for nature and increasing one's awe of creation. As noted earlier, many participants recognized, through their prayer practice, a greater awe and appreciation for all of God's creation. Within Christian spirituality, a renewed interconnection with nature can enhance one's sense of inner peace and awareness of God's eternal power and divine nature (Romans 1:20). Theologian and Roman Catholic Priest Emmanuel Duke (2020) insisted that ecological spirituality goes beyond connecting with nature to attitudes and a way of life that holds a deep appreciation for God's gift of nature. Additionally, recognizing a greater connection with one's natural environment can contribute to efforts related to the conservation and sustainability of creation. It has been said that 'nature does not need humankind; it is human beings that need nature'.[14] An important element for Christians, within their 'eco-consciousness', is

[14] Duke (2020:34).

that humans need to develop a greater sense of integration with and care for nature. In an integrated way within the self, participants recognized that their environmental, social, and personal well-being strengthened their self-transcendence towards God.

Spiritual Well-Being

Within their self-transcendence towards God, participants also recognized a greater sense of spiritual well-being. Although this grounded theory study depended on participants' meanings emerging directly from the data, and not from other evaluation methods or measures, participants reflected on aspects of spiritual well-being that resonated with items on the SHALOM spiritual well-being questionnaire and evaluation.[15] For example, participants' data emerged with meanings of spiritual well-being recognized as growing more spiritual, living with greater awareness of their identity as a child of God, recognizing God as loving, opening to God's presence, and allowing the Spirit to work in their life. These aspects supported a growing sense of spiritual well-being in the lived experience of long-term Christian Contemplative Prayer practitioners, serving to strengthen their relationship and sense of oneness with God. Integration of the whole embodied person – body, mind, and spirit – was an important element of the Christian Contemplative Prayer practitioner's spirituality and increasing well-being. This important role of one's whole embodied being was illustrated in the meanings supporting participants' lived experience

[15] In his lived experience component of SHALOM, Fisher (2010:209) delineated the Transcendental domain, within spiritual well-being, in accordance with 'personal relationship with the Divine/God; worship of the Creator; oneness with God; peace with God; prayer life'. This further related to one's personal, communal, environmental, and transcendental well-being.

of Christian Contemplative Prayer and well-being in their life.

Embodiment

Embodied Spiritual Practices

Integration of body, mind, and spirit is an important aspect of one's Christian spirituality. The initial awareness of the important role of the body in Christian Contemplative Prayer became one of the building blocks for the importance of embodiment within this prayer practice. Through the Incarnation, Jesus exemplified wholeness and an embodied existence unmarred by sin. Embodiment needed to be understood as it permeated the Christian Contemplative Prayer experience of divine presence and one's desire for embodied wholeness.

While various scholars support the importance of recognizing the body and its role in one's Christian spirituality, the church has often neglected this reality. This spiritual perspective has been negatively influenced by Platonic philosophy, which maintained that the human soul, being of divine origin, is inherently good, while the human body, being of earthly origin, is inherently bad. This has led to a picture of salvation relating to the release of the spirit from the sinful body, causing some Christian thinking to maintain the idea that the body is a hindrance to spiritual growth and is considered the root of human sinfulness. However, elements of embodiment supported the practice of Christian Contemplative Prayer in a holistic developmental way related to *Embodied Self*; *Embodied in Christian Community*; *Embodied Space*; and participants' *Embodiment in God*.

From each of these perspectives, the body was recognized as an essential aspect within this prayer practice, and as Christian scholar and psychologist Elizabeth Hall (2010:173) contended, 'all of the spiritual disciplines are done in the body and with the body'. It is not the goal of this book to engage in the debate over embodiment, but rather, to generate a theory based on participant data that theorizes the long-term practitioners' lived Christian Contemplative Prayer experience. From participants' meanings and perspectives, embodiment helped to support their holistic development and well-being within their Christian Contemplative Prayer practice.

Embodiment, Imago Dei, and the Incarnation

The body is a vital part of what it means to be a human being, and is equally important from a Christian perspective. Studying the embodied lived experience can lead to a greater understanding of the need to integrate more fully an awareness of the body's role in one's Christian spirituality and spiritual practices. As a lived experience of Christian Contemplative Prayer, long-term practitioners pray with the entirety of their being: body, mind, and spirit.

Christian theologians affirm that human beings were created in God's image, *imago Dei*. In building upon the understanding and words of Aquinas related to *imago Dei,* the body, mind, and spirit act together with one another; therefore, human beings' longing towards God is done with body, mind, and spirit in concert. This was recognized within Christian Contemplative Prayer practice; the practitioners' believed that their embodied, unified intention towards God allowed for a union with God in contemplation involving the totality of the embodied self.

This embodied experience also recognized the importance of the body as sanctioned through the Incarnation, which is the highest endorsement of the human body there is. Christ came to this earth in an actual human body so that he might bring salvation and deliverance to *our* body. Christians must look to Jesus' model of embodied existence unmarred by sin. In Jesus, the dualism of body and mind is integrated into the whole of human existence of body, mind, and spirit. The *imago Dei* and the Incarnational aspects of the Christian's being animate the lived experience of Christian Contemplative Prayer: the union of the divine with humanity.

Embodied Self

As a bodily experience, the totality of one's being is engaged in this prayer practice. Participants insisted that the more 'relaxed' the physical posture, or subservient to the process of intention on God, the better the participants were able to posture themselves mentally, releasing thoughts and resting in contemplative union with God. The body has a role in bringing practitioners to a physically relaxed state, which can help induce a mentally and spiritually relaxed embodied state. For some, this was beginning in a restful, sitting posture, but for others there was a need for kinaesthetic activity to quieten their body in eventual silence and contemplative union with God.

Embodied in Christian Community

Christians, like all human beings, are not merely disembodied spirits. Humans were created to be embodied beings not separated from their bodies, but rather personifying a created wholeness. The body is an integral part of one's sociality and spirituality. Their lived experience of Christian spirituality is interconnected in and through their bodies, both individually and socially. Participants expressed various ways that this practice embodied them within their Christian community, and they felt the group's experience as the Body of Christ often involved a certain holistic state of consciousness and spiritual unity.

Within this relational interface, elements of psychologist Mihaly Csikszentmihalyi's research on *flow* (Nakamura & Csikszentmihalyi 2002), and social phenomenologist Alfred Schütz's (1951) work on *inner time* both bring understanding to participants' experiences within Christian Contemplative Prayer. Psychology scholars Jeanne Nakamura and Mihalyi Csikszentmihalyi (2002), utilizing the concept of flow, have provided an understanding of individuals' lived experience as they are involved in an activity. Additionally, Schütz's insights on the flux of experiences in inner time have enhanced our understanding of relationships within communication. Although their work did not address religious or spiritual experiences specifically, the focus was on the relating of individuals in their embodied presence together.

Csikszentmihalyi described such holistic consciousness as he developed the concept of flow. He used this term to illustrate the intensely dynamic aspect of an experience in which the individual controlled their actions, yet they perceived little distinction between themselves, others, and their environment. The engaged individual remained actively assimilated in their embodied self and wholly embodied within their activity and their surroundings. Csikszentmihalyi demonstrated how activities requiring high levels of physical and mental concentration (for example, chess masters and rock climbers) can require participants to engage in a state of flow. This involved a certain holistic state of consciousness during these activities. This aspect of flow further supported practitioners' focused intention and attention in their Christian Contemplative Prayer. In flow, one did not lose a conscious awareness of their surroundings, but rather became absorbed within their embodied presence in their environment with others, and in the case of Christian Contemplative Prayer, one further became embodied in the presence of God. Sociologist James Spickard (1991) argued that lived experiences are the subjective aspect of religious gatherings, and these experiences were deeply social as they were shared in the *flow of time*. The unifying experience of Christian Contemplative prayer enhanced the shared social and spiritual experience of this prayer time.

Yet, another important element within the embodiment of Christian community was recognized in the integrated aspect of the Body of Christ. As theologian Debra Reagan insisted, the profound awareness of recognizing that Christians, as embodied selves, were also corporeal or bodily members of the Body of Christ is a vital aspect of the Christian's faith and the sociality of their lived experiences within Christian Contemplative Prayer. Reagan (2013:57) further argued that '[t]he Body of Christ in 1 Corinthians 12:12–27 is an empty metaphor without the bodies that constitute it', and that Christians were called to 'enflesh' the metaphor of the Body of Christ. While it was important to recognize the embodied self within Christian Contemplative Prayer, as Hall (2010) argued, individualism and a focus only on one's individual relationship with God, de-emphasized one's embodied lived experience within the broader community of the Body of Christ. Beyond the social science theories, there is an influence of the connective power of the Holy Spirit within the Body of Christ, which also went *beyond words*. As Hall contends, both the physical body and the gathered Body of Christ were recognized as a sacred place of God's presence, a sacred place that may defy description and embody the spiritual experience. This element of Christian Contemplative Prayer embodied in the Christian community became a sacred space for the participants, also.

Embodied Space

Another important aspect for long-term Christian Contemplative Prayer practitioners was related to their embodiment within their prayer space. For example, a method involving contemplative photography, contemplative gardening, or contemplative physical exercise might include a space that requires a significant amount of area for locomotion, yet one was embodied fully in that space. In contrast, such methods as Centering Prayer, contemplative art, or contemplative journaling might require a minimal amount of locomotion. This physically embodied space could also be reduced to a chair, a place to kneel, or a place to lie down; yet, for all methods of Christian Contemplative Prayer within their sacred space, participants expressed that the ultimate intention was stillness and silence in contemplative union with God within that space.

As participants reflected on their concept of space within their Christian Contemplative Prayer practice, they further referenced a meaningful place of union with God that is often familiar; a place that one longed to be; a place of rest; a wonderful space with God that felt safe and enclosed. Similar to Psychologist Victor Counted and Professor of Religion and Mental Health Hetty Zock's (2019) concept of *Place Spirituality*, Christian Contemplative Prayer practitioners appeared to recognize their embodied prayer space as a place to be with God and from which to 'leave' and live out their faith (with God), and then a place to return to the security, safety, and love of God and rest in contemplative union with God. Practitioners did not speak of staying in that Christian Contemplative Prayer embodied space consistently, yet it was a space to come and go, a *therapeutic space* which enhanced opportunities for rest and relaxation in God.

Embodied in God

Within their lived experience and self-transcendence towards God, practitioners recognized a fuller awareness of their embodied union with God in contemplation. An important element of this awareness was found within the complex concept of *interiority*, which reflects being present to oneself. Interiority supports an intimacy with God involving the depths of one's holistic being. This is the heart of Christian Contemplative Prayer; an embodied spiritual intimacy with God in one's innermost being.

Practitioners' prayer practice was also deeply embodied in God's love and presence, which helped further develop a healthy love of self, others, creation, and God. The importance of this love affirms the *imago Dei* in such a way that the body is not separate from the rest of one's being. It is an embodied experience. For many participants, embodiment in God was further recognized within the Incarnation (John 1:14). God became embodied in Jesus and accepted the limitations of a human body. Christian Contemplative Prayer helps humans to recognize their embodiedness within their limitless God, yet with all their own human limitations.

Participants recognized another aspect of their embodied nature in God as the temple of God. Scriptural testimony of God's temple among human beings was established in 1 Corinthians 3:16: 'Do you not know that you yourselves are God's temple and that God's Spirit dwells in your midst?' Scripture further affirms the human body in 1 Corinthians 6:13–20 with the admonition that the body is 'for the Lord, and the Lord for the body' (v.13b), and similarly the rhetorical question Paul asks: 'Do you not know that your bodies are members of Christ himself?' (v.15a). In these ways, the embodied Christian is to be a sacred place within which the Spirit of God's presence resides. Through their Christian Contemplative Prayer practice, these scriptural teachings became more of a recognized reality as practitioners referenced carrying the temple within them. Hall (2010:174) insisted that 'spiritual disciplines allow us as whole, embodied people, to show God's indwelling presence – His glory – in His temple'.

Embodied in God is a multi-faceted, complex, experiential relationship within the love and presence of God. It envelopes the mystery of God within the practitioner, in the depth of their interiority. Its importance is reflected in the Incarnation of God in Christ and the value of the created embodied Christian as the temple of God; that is God within the Christian Contemplative Prayer practitioner. It further reflects the theological emphasis on the role of the body in glorifying God – nurturing the understanding that God can be experienced within one's own physicality.

Practitioners' growing awareness of God's presence in their life, and their embodied union with God also created a greater appreciation for unceasing prayer in their life. It was their growing consciousness of God's embodied presence in their Christian Contemplative Prayer practice that helped them develop an increasing realization of God with them throughout the day, which in turn promoted a greater awareness of praying without ceasing. The long-term Christian Contemplative Prayer practitioners in this study realized their embodied selves, their embodiment within a Christian community, their embodiment within their prayer space, and their embodiment in God as they rested in contemplative union with God.

Diagrammatic Summary

Diagramming Christian Contemplative Prayer and Spirituality

The interrelation of Christian Contemplative Prayer, well-being, and embodiment is graphically presented in Figure 2 overleaf.

This figure demonstrates the enveloping aspect of Christian Spirituality in orientating this study within the grounded theory analysis of participants' data. For illustrative purposes, two aspects of Christian Spirituality have been combined into one: lived experience and uniqueness of the individual lived experience being represented in the diagram by *unique lived experience.* The orientating aspect of Christian Spirituality is illustrated by the encircling chevrons in the diagram. Within the circle are the various embodiment aspects of Christian Contemplative Prayer, with each one located within the previous one, yet all interrelated as indicated by the concentric dashed lines. At the very core of the illustration is the practitioner's embodied, holistic well-being: personal, communal, environmental, and spiritual. This sense of well-being within one's

Figure 2 presents the Christian Contemplative Prayer practice and its interrelation within Christian Spirituality as recognized in the lived experience, conscious process, holistic development, self-transcendence towards God, and the uniqueness of the individual lived experience.

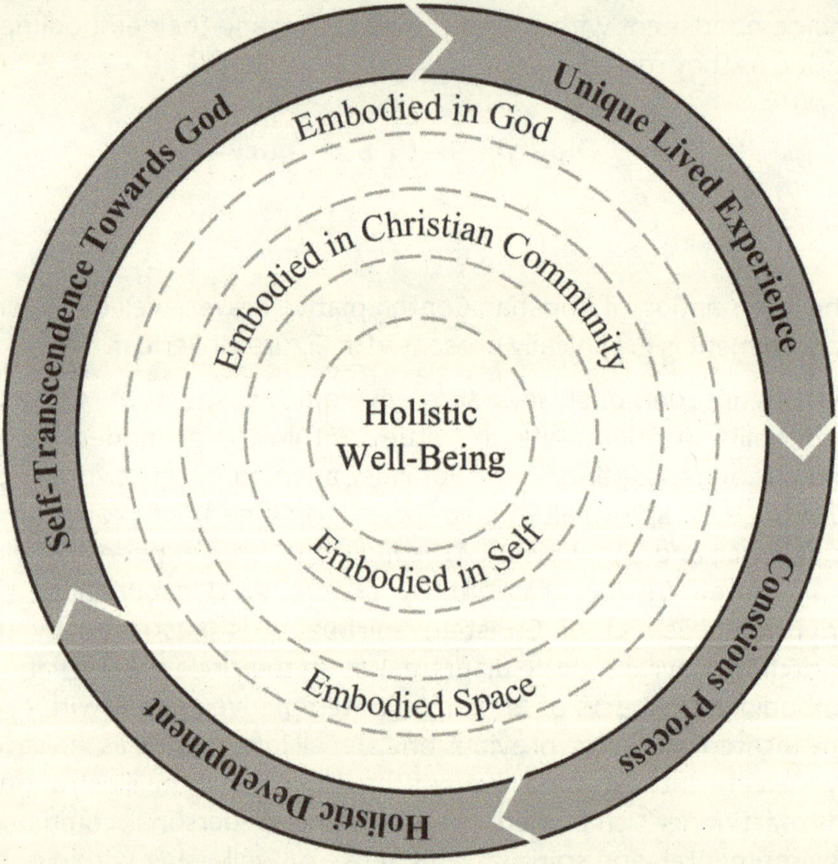

self, with others, the environment, and God is at the core of Christian Contemplative Prayer.

Diagramming Christian Contemplative Prayer, Embodiment, and Well-Being

The second theoretical framework, illustrated in Figure 3 overleaf, represents the integrated connections that emerged in this study of Christian Contemplative Prayer. This framework reflects the interconnection between Christian Contemplative Prayer, well-being, and embodiment conceptual categories, and their relation to relevant theories. It also illustrates the processes by which multiple categories inform and shape the long-term practitioner's lived experience within their embodied Christian Contemplative Prayer practice. Emerging through the data, the category of embodiment developed an analytic power to help explain this research and its interconnections. Rather than just a descriptive awareness of well-being, experienced by participants, aspects of embodiment helped to create a coherent, integrated picture of Christian Contemplative Prayer, well-being, and embodiment.

Christian Contemplative Prayer – *Promoted* by one's pursuit of both God's presence and embodied wholeness in one's self. Within one's practice, there was a potential discovery of various methods of Christian Contemplative Prayer, which allowed one to enter a place of stillness and silence in God's presence. Practitioners then recognized that their prayer practice *influenced* their various states of holistic well-being (body, mind, and spirit).

Figure 3 presents the dynamic relation of the long-term Christian Contemplative Prayer practitioners' realization of physical, mental, and spiritual well-being, integrated within their embodied lived experience of their long-term Christian Contemplative Prayer practice.

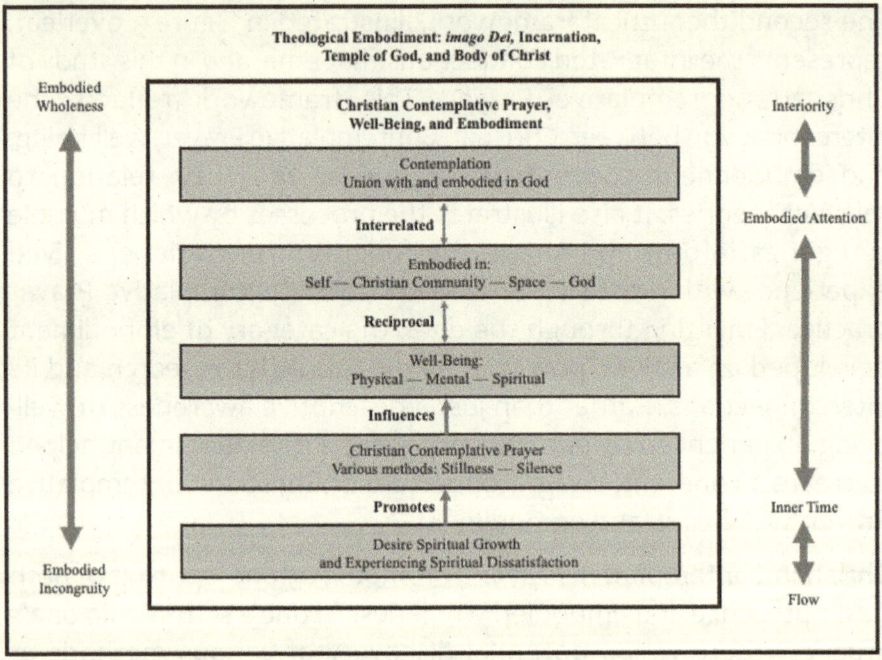

Well-Being: Physical, Mental, and Spiritual – Among Christian Contemplative Prayer practitioners there was a sense of a *reciprocal* effect of increasingly positive well-being and different aspects of embodiment ongoing within one's realization of embodied wholeness and contemplation in union with God.

Embodied in Self, in Christian Community, in Space, and in God – Participants recognized the ways in which their prayer practice was facilitated through aspects of embodiment. Within the concept of embodied self, participants realized that they did not pray in a disembodied way, but rather their embodied self was involved in Christian Contemplative Prayer, giving them a greater sense of wholeness in God's presence. Embodied in Christian community helped to explain the interconnected aspects of this spiritual practice through a sense of unity and oneness with others. Embodied space helped to develop a fuller aspect of the way in which the place of prayer played a role in practitioners' prayer practice, in the facilitation of prayer time, and in aspects of wholeness. Embodied in God reflected the way in which the participants' prayer time was *interrelated* with God's presence.

Contemplation: Union with God – It was this *interrelatedness* of embodiment that helped to create an awareness of contemplation in union with God; the contemplative resting place of this spiritual practice as embodied in self, Christian community, an embodied space, and contemplative union with God.

Theological Embodiment: *Imago Dei,* Incarnation, Temple of God, and Body of Christ – Concepts of theological embodiment were integrated with participants' scriptural understandings of the *imago Dei,* Incarnation, temple of God, and the Body of Christ.

Flow, Inner Time, Embodied Attention, Interiority – There is a progression of flow and inner time developing within the practitioner and their practice of Christian Contemplative Prayer. This continues to progress in a process of embodied attention and aspects of interiority.

Embodied Incongruity towards Embodied Wholeness – The Christian's embodied incongruity helps to create an openness and desire for Christian Contemplative Prayer. Throughout their long-term practice of Christian Contemplative Prayer, practitioners continue to develop a sense of greater embodied wholeness. This wholeness is a part of their increasing holistic well-being within this embodied prayer practice.

6. Conclusion

This book has illuminated the lived experience of long-term Christian Contemplative Prayer practitioners and the interrelated aspects of well-being and embodiment. It has helped to substantiate Christian Contemplative Prayer scholars who have suggested Christian Contemplative Prayer's influence on well-being. The research findings, presented in Chapter 4, have highlighted participants' eudaemonic sense of well-being and embodiment within this prayer practice. This has helped to provide an understanding of Christian Contemplative Prayer's influence on holistic well-being, and the embodied individuals' experiences of growth in their interior life related to such aspects as peace, authenticity, kindness, centredness, and patience. There was concurrently a greater sense of one's true self as practitioners continued their long-term prayer practice and its associated contemplative union in God. Increasing development of one's true self was also recognized within their emotional healing. The findings further offered a contribution to the ways in which Christian Contemplative Prayer influences not only individuals' personal well-being (leading to embodied wholeness) but also their communal, environmental, and spiritual well-being.

Participants' increasing positive relations with others led to greater communal well-being. This was realized not only in relationships but also in the way that others recognized positive changes within the practitioner and the practitioner's desire to restore difficult relationships. Participants' well-being was also extended towards and within all of creation. This connection with nature seemed to help support inner peace, a strengthening of their relationship with God and nature, and a deepening of practitioners' appreciation and awe of the natural world. This book (and the more extensive thesis on which this book is based) explored the processes that supported well-being within Christian Contemplative Prayer. Participants' increasing spiritual well-being, greater awareness of God's presence, and growing relationship with God were all part of their long-term Christian Contemplative Prayer lived experience. It is one of a few studies to explore Christian Contemplative Prayer and well-being specifically among long-term practitioners, and offers one of the first grounded theories in the relationship of not only well-being within this prayer practice but also the interrelatedness of embodiment, well-being, and Christian Contemplative Prayer.

Embodiment has been further delineated into four aspects within this prayer practice: *Embodied Self*, *Embodied in Christian Community*, *Embodied Space*, and *Embodied in God*. This research further highlighted the importance of the Incarnation, the communal Body of Christ, the individual as the temple of God, and the recognition of *imago Dei* as important theological concepts integrated into embodiment within Christian Contemplative Prayer.

This research helps advance insights into embodied prayer practice and its influence on long-term practitioners' well-being. The increasing understanding of Christian Contemplative Prayer, well-being, and embodiment can benefit Christian Contemplative Prayer scholars, Christian leaders who teach Christian Contemplative Prayer or who wish to understand it better, Christian Contemplative Prayer practitioners, and Christians who do not yet practise or understand Christian Contemplative Prayer. Greater clarity of this practice can open doors of understanding for the global church community, helping Christian traditions and individuals alike to better appreciate and potentially embrace this embodied prayer practice within their own spiritual disciplines. In this way they can comprehend, participate, and benefit from this embodied Christian prayer practice in their relational understanding of God.

7. Author's Note

Christian Contemplative Prayer is a relatively new practice in my own lived experience of Christian spirituality; a prayer practice that has begun only since the start of this study. I do not believe I am experiencing this prayer practice and its influence in the same way as long-term Christian Contemplative Prayer practitioners, nor would I expect to. But I do believe I am experiencing contemplation within this prayer practice and am becoming more aware of its influence as expressed by the participants in this study. I recognize that it will continue to be a positive part of my own spiritual discipline and practice for years to come. Only then might I realize a fuller impact of Christian Contemplative Prayer in my own embodied lived experience of Christian spirituality. Through this study and my related self-implicating experience, I am grateful for having learned in depth about Christian Contemplative Prayer from such faithful practitioners. To God be the glory.

Bibliography

Anonymous (2017) *The Cloud of Unknowing*. Edited by Evelyn Underhill. Kentucky.

Bourgeault, Cynthia (2016) *The Heart of Centering Prayer*. Colorado: Shambhala.

Butler, E. Cuthbert (2011) *Western Mysticism*. Vol. III. Routledge Library of Religion and Mysticism. London and New York: Routledge: Taylor and Francis Group

Counted, Victor and Zock, Hetty (2019) 'Place Spirituality: An Attachment Perspective' *Archive for the Psychology of Religion* 41, no. 1: 12–25. https://doi.org/10.1177/0084672419833448.

Duke, Emmanuel (2020) 'From Christian Spirituality to Eco-Friendliness' *International Journal of Humanities and Innovation* 3, no. 1: 34–38.

Fisher, John (2010) 'Development and Application of a Spiritual Well-Being Questionnaire Called SHALOM' *Religions* 1: 105–21. https://doi.org/10.3390/rel1010105.

Frenette, David (2008) 'Three Contemplative Waves' In *Spirituality, Contemplation & Transformation*, 9–55. Brooklyn, New York: Lantern Books.

Hall, Elizabeth (2010) 'What Are Bodies for? An Integrated Examination of Embodiment' *Christian Scholar's Review* 39, no. 2: 159–75.

Heiler, Friedrich (1950) *Prayer: A Study in the History and Psychology of Religion*. Oxford: Galaxy Books

Merton, Thomas (1960) *The Wisdom of the Desert*. New York, New York: New Directions.

Nakamura, Jeanne and Csikszentmihalyi, Mihaly (2002) 'The Concept of Flow' In *Handbook of Positive Psychology*, by Snyder, C.R.; Shane Lopez, 89–105. Oxford Library of Psychology Series. New York: Oxford University Press.

Reagan, Debra (2013) 'Reclaiming the Body for Faith' *Interpretation: A Journal of Bible and Theology* 67, no. 1: 42–57. https://doi.org/10.1177/0020964312463331.

Ryan, Thomas (1995) *Prayer of Heart & Body*. New Jersey: Paulist press.

Schütz, Alfred (1951) 'Making Music Together' *Social Research* 18, no. 1: 76–97.

Ziemke, Tom (2003) 'What's That Thing Called Embodiment?' *UC Merced: Proceedings of the Annual Meeting of the Cognitive Science Society*, 1305–10.

Further Reading

Allison, Gregg (2009) 'Toward a Theology of Human Embodiment' *Southern Baptist Journal of Theology* 13, no. 2: 4–17.

Coe, John, and Strobel, Kyle (2019) *Embracing Contemplation*. Illinois: InterVarsity Press.

Connelly, Lynne (2016) 'Trustworthiness in Qualitative Research' *Medsurg Nursing* 25, no. 6: 435–36.

D'Angelo, Diego (2020) 'The Phenomenology of Embodied Attention' *Phenomenology and the Cognitive Sciences* 19: 961–78. https://doi.org/10.1007/s11097-019-09637-2.

Danaher, James (2011) *Contemplative Prayer*. Oregon: Cascade Books.

Dreyer, Elizabeth (2007) *Holy Power, Holy Presence: Rediscovering Medieval Metaphors for the Holy Spirit*. New York: Paulist.

Dunn, Marilynn (2003) *The Emergence of Monasticism: From the Desert Fathers to the Middle Ages*. Oxford: Blackwell Publishing.

Ferguson, Jane; Willemsen, Eleanor and Castañeto, MayLynn (2010a) 'Centering Prayer as a Healing Response to Everyday

Stress: A Psychological and Spiritual Process' *Pastoral Psychology*, no. 59: 305–29. https://doi.org/10.1007/s11089-009-0225-7.

Ferguson, Jane (2010b). 'Contemplative Practices in Action: Spirituality, Meditation, and Health' edited by Plante, Thomas. 60–77. California: Praeger

Finney, John and Malony, H. Newton (1985a). 'Empirical Studies of Christian Prayer: A Review of the Literature.' *Journal of Psychology & Theology* 13, no. 2: 104–15.

Finney, John and Malony, H. Newton (1985b) 'Contemplative Prayer and Its Use in Psychotherapy: A Theoretical Model' *Journal of Psychology & Theology* 13, no. 3: 172–81. https://doi.org/10.1177/009164718501300302.

Finney, John and Malony, H. Newton (1985c) 'An Empirical Study of Contemplative Prayer as an Adjunct to Psychotherapy' *Journal of Psychology & Theology* 13, no. 4: 284–90.

Flusberg, Stephen (2016) 'Embodiment and Embodied Cognition' *Oxford Bibliographies*, https://doi.org/10.1093/OBO/9780199828340-0023.

Fox, Jesse; Gutierrez, Daniel; Haas, Jessica; Braganza, Dinesh and Berger, Christine (2015) 'A Phenomenological Investigation of Centering Prayer Using Conventional Content Analysis' *Pastoral Psychology*, no. 64: 803–25. https://doi.org/10.1007/s11089-015-0657-1.

Fox, Jesse; Gutierrez, Daniel; Haas, Jessica and Durnford, Stephanie (2016) 'Centering Prayer's Effects on Psycho-Spiritual Outcomes:

A Pilot Outcome Study' *Mental Health, Religion & Culture* 19, no. 4: 379–92. https://doi.org/10.1080/13674676.2016.1203299.

Frohlich, Mary (2001) 'Spiritual Discipline, Discipline of Spirituality: Revisiting Questions of Definition and Method' *Spiritus: A Journal of Christian Spirituality*, 1, no. 1: 65–78. https://doi.org/10.1353/scs.2001.0009.

Frohlich, Mary (2019) 'Spirit, Spirituality, and Contemplative Method' *Mysterion* 2, no. 12: 129–39.

Greenwood, Tracey and Delgado, Teresa (2013) 'A Journey Toward Wholeness, a Journey to God: Physical Fitness as Embodied Spirituality' 52: 941–54. https://doi.org/10.1007/s10943-011-9546-9.

Gutierrez, Daniel; Fox, Jesse and Wood, Andrew (2015) 'Center, Light, and Sound: The Psychological Benefits of Three Distinct Meditative Practices' *Counseling and Values* 60: 234–47. https://doi.org/10.1002/cvj.12016.

Johnson, Mary E.; Ann M. Dose; Wesley Petersen; Mashele Huschka; Mary Gallenberg; Teri Britt Pipe; Prema Peethambaram; Jeff Sloan; and Marlene Frost (2009) 'Centering Prayer for Women Receiving Chemotherapy for Recurrent Ovarian Cancer: A Pilot Study.' *Oncology Nursing Forum* 36, no. 4: 421–28.

Keating, Thomas (1996) *Open Mind, Open Heart: The Contemplative Dimension of the Gospel*. New ed. with updates. New York: Continuum.

Keating, Thomas (2007) *Invitation to Love: The Way of Christian Contemplation*. New York: Continuum.

Keating, Thomas, ed. (2008) *Spirituality, Contemplation, & Transformation: Writings on Centering Prayer*. New York: Lantern Books.

Keating, Thomas (2009) *Intimacy with God: An Introduction to Centering Prayer*. New York: The Crossroads Publishing Co.

Keller, David (2008) 'Reading Living Water: The Integral Place of Contemplative Prayer in Christian Transformation' In *Spirituality, Contemplation, & Transformation*. New York: Lantern Books.

Knabb, Joshua (2012) 'Centering Prayer as Alternative to Mindfulness-Based Cognitive Therapy for Depression Relapse Prevention' *Journal of Religion and Health*, no. 51: 908–24. https://doi.org/10.1007?s10943-010-9404-1.

Kruse, Joshua (2012) 'Differential Effects of Centering Prayer and Progressive Muscle Relaxation as an Intervention for Anxiety Reduction' Doctor of Philosophy, Biola University.

Kuiper, Judith (2004) 'The Experience of Centering Prayer: A Heuristic Inquiry' Doctor of Philosophy, The Union Institute and University.

Laird, Martin (2005) 'The "Open Country Whose Name Is Prayer": Apophasis, Deconstruction, and Contemplative Practice' *Modern Theology* 21, no. 1: 141–55. https://doi.org/10.1111/j.1468-0025.2005.00279.x.

Laird, Martin (2006) *Into the Silent Land: A Guide to the Christian Practice of Contemplation*. Oxford; New York: Oxford University Press.

Lysne, Carol (2012) 'An Exploratory Study of the Power of a Mantra Form of Contemplative Prayer to Awaken the Presence of the Transcendent in Daily Living' Dissertation, Institute of Transpersonal Psychology.

Main, John (2006) *Word into Silence*. Edited by Freeman, Laurence. Norwich: Canterbury Press.

Obbard, Ruth, ed. (2007) *Medieval Women Mystics*. New York: New City Press.

Paintner, Christine ed. (2012) *Desert Fathers and Mothers: Early Christian Wisdom Sayings, Annotated & Explained*. Quality pbk. ed. Skylight Illuminations Series. Vermont: SkyLight Paths Publishing.

Rolheiser, Ronald (2013) *Prayer: Our Deepest Longing*. Ohio, USA: Franciscan Media.

Willard, Dallas and Simpson, Dan (2005) *Revolution of Character: Discovering Christ's Pattern for Spiritual Transformation*. Canada: NavPress.

Appendix 1: The Method of Centering Prayer

(Adapted from:

Bourgeault, C. (2016) *The Heart of Centering Prayer*. Colorado: Shambhala.

Keating, T (1996) *Open Mind, Open Heart: The Contemplative Dimension of the Gospel*. New ed. with updates. New York: Continuum.)

Step One: Choose a word which can be used to ground one's intention towards the consent of God's presence and action during Centering Prayer time. This word is not a mantra. It is simply a way to help one return in a receptive way to God's presence. This is not a word to focus on, just to help you return to a receptive awareness.

Step Two: Choose a place to sit that will be conducive to exterior silence, to help support the interior silence of Centering Prayer. This is supported by these words of Jesus: 'But when you pray, go into your room, close the door and pray to your Father, who is unseen' (Matt 6:6). For Centering Prayer practitioners, the inner room is that space deep within, away from the cares and chaos of the external world where one can meet with God in secret and in the most intimate ways.

Step Three: As thoughts come, they are simply released in a way that opens up one to be receptive to the presence of God in the stillness and quiet. One can acknowledge any thoughts and then let them go.

Step Four: When distractions arise, simply release them and return to your receptive awareness.

Step Five: Continue to be open in a loving and faithful way to the presence of God, and the awakening of your true self in God.

Appendix 2: In Their Own Words

Participant interviews produced countless hours worth of insightful data about Christian Contemplative Prayer. Presenting all of the interview data would not be possible in this appendix; however, I wanted to present just a glimpse of participants' own words and thoughts about their long-term prayer practice.

It was just like being in the sacred space... (P1)

[I]n my daily life, I can feel God's presence much stronger than I could before. (P2)

We do contemplative prayer [...]and it is for all of humanity, all of creation. (P3)

I'm listening to God and that's what I think Centering Prayer really is. (P4)

[I]n terms of healing and Centering Prayer... opening, being open to God's healing love... so healing. (P5)

[T]hrough my Centering Prayer, I've just grown to that conviction that I'm a beloved child of God. (P6)

I find that you can't really explain it because it's beyond words, and words can only point to it. (P7)

So, I believe in Centering Prayer as a healing practice... (P8)

[T]he letting go in this moment. I consent to the work that God is doing. (P9)

I don't know how specifically I can describe it [Christian Contemplative Prayer]. (P10)

[T]he sitting and the groundedness brought me back into relationship with my body, which was necessary for me to really entertain healing that would last. (P11)

It is an openness to God's presence. (P12)

But I will say, in a group, it can be more powerful. (P13)

Doing Centering Prayer and learning about letting go and living in the moment. I have learned to feel that this moment could be the best because that is where God is. (P14)

From a theoretical perspective, the embodied space [of Christian Contemplative Prayer] was recognized as an intentional space, that could act in a sense as a tent, and could also be held for others to embody. (P15)

I think my prayer practices for me are generally based around movement. (P16)

When you sit in contemplative prayer, your mind is active, in a different kind of a way. Right? Not an active way with our brains thinking, but it's still engaged in God's presence. (P17)

I used to think of prayer as a little request-making. But I think the emphasis with contemplative prayer is about listening. (P18)

Of course, God is in the silence. (P19)

It also has a curative process on my health. (P20)

I think the sense of profound stillness comes more easily and quickly and it arises more readily in a group. (P21)

Contemplation is putting yourself in God's gaze and being totally open to whatever he sends... (P22)

So, I think a big impact is the awareness, prayer without ceasing. (P23)

Contemplative prayer is about sitting in God's presence, that pure presence. (P24)

I started giving myself permission, that there was more than one way to seek God. (P25)

I begin with lectio divina with a group, and then it becomes easy to introduce [them to] Centering Prayer. (P26)

[S]ink into divine presence. It's not a cure-all, but it does help me to cope if things go wrong, either in my body or externally. (P27)

I think embodiment is huge. It is a bodily experience, and that is what contemplation or the contemplative experience is part of. (P28)

It is strange that I had to live so long without realizing anything about contemplative prayer. It has to do with the love of God, the incarnational [...] Unfortunately, it is the best kept secret. (P29)

So, the things I do in my body set me up to be in that silent space. (P30)

There is a time and place for prayer and so on, but it is a lived experience. It becomes the filter that you filter everything else through. (P31)

I have been in a wonderful space with God, what else is there? I have just been with you [God], what else needs to happen or be said? (P32)

I believe there are so many ways [of Christian Contemplative prayer], just as there are other people. (P33)

Some contemplative and meditative prayer practices seek to transcend, overcome, or tame the body. Others invite the body to participate and to offer the wisdom it carries in its physicality. (P34)

God is not a problem to figure out. So, for me, contemplative practice has helped that sense that I just want to be with God. (P35)

If you ask me to explain it, I am not sure I can. You know it is a mystery, but I sensed God was doing something in the Centering Prayer practice or the contemplative prayer practice. (P36)